FR. MARK TOUPS

Rejoice!

An Advent Pilgrimage into
the Heart of Scripture

Year B

ASCENSION

West Chester, Pennsylvania

Nihil Obstat:	Reverend S. Brice Higginbotham
	Censor Librorum
	June 26, 2023
Imprimatur:	+Most Reverend Mario E. Dorsonville, STL, DMin
	Bishop of Houma-Thibodaux
	June 27, 2023

The *Nihil Obstat* and *Imprimatur* are official declarations that a book or pamphlet is free of doctrinal or moral error. No implication is contained therein that those who have granted the *Nihil Obstat* or *Imprimatur* agree with the content, opinions, or statements expressed.

Ascension
PO Box 1990
West Chester, PA 19380
1-800-376-0520
ascensionpress.com

Cover art: Mike Moyers (*Gloria* © 2023 Mike Moyers, Franklin, TN).

Interior art: Mike Moyers (*Shine on Us*, *A Voice Calling*, *Released*, *Let It Be*, *The Word* © 2023 Mike Moyers, Franklin, TN).

ISBN: 978-1-954882-26-3 (paperback)
ISBN: 978-1-954882-27-0 (e-book)

Printed in the United States of America

CONTENTS

PREFACE

Welcome to Advent. Welcome to *Rejoice!*

For those of you reading, I would like to welcome you to my favorite liturgical season. If this is your first experience of *Rejoice!*, allow me to share my hope that the Lord will bless you beyond your expectations as we prepare for Christmas.

There are three things I would like to emphasize in this introduction, three things that will help you appreciate what God wants to do in your life this Advent.

First, the theme of this year's *Rejoice!* is learning to hear God's voice. This singular theme is woven throughout the book. This year, we ask the Lord to speak to us. The meditations are specifically and intentionally written to help you learn how to hear the voice of God. While in years past we told the story of Advent, this year we are seeking to learn from Mary and Joseph how to hear the voice of God as they did.

Second, we are using the Sunday Mass readings for Year B as our guide this year. Throughout Advent, the theme of learning to hear God's voice will provide the pace and movement of each week, and the readings will give us insights into the theme. On the first days of the week, Sunday through Wednesday, we consider words from that Sunday's readings. Then, starting on Thursday, we look ahead to the readings that await us at next Sunday's Mass. My hope is that, as we introduce you to next weekend's readings *before* Sunday, you will be better able to appreciate those readings *on* Sunday.

Third, I need to remind you that the most important voice we listen to is the voice of the Lord. The purpose of each day's meditation is to prepare you to hear God's voice in the spiritual exercise for the day. The meditation that precedes the "For Your Prayer" prompt supports your prayer; it does not exist as a separate entity. My job as an author is to help you hear the voice of the Creator. Please make time to pray with the "For Your Prayer" prompt every day instead of just reading the meditation.

It is a joy for us to be together. I *rejoice!*

I very much look forward to what God will do in our lives this Advent. Let us ask the Lord to bless our ears so that over the coming weeks, we can hear his voice.

Fr. Mark Toups

GETTING THE MOST OUT OF *REJOICE!*

The book you have in your hands is an Advent prayer journal with daily meditations by Fr. Mark Toups and artwork by Mike Moyers. It is the sixth in the ongoing series of *Rejoice!* journals from Ascension. Earlier journals in this series are *Advent Meditations with Mary*, *Advent Meditations with Joseph*, *Advent Meditations with the Holy Family*, *Finding Yourself in the Advent Story*, and *An Advent Pilgrimage into the Heart of Scripture, Year A*.

This journal provides daily meditations based on the Sunday readings for Advent, Year B. We invite you to take a journey with them into the heart of the Advent season.

Community

Rejoice! journals are designed to be used by parishes, small groups, and individuals as they prepare for Christmas. Community is a key component of the journey to holiness, and Advent provides an excellent opportunity to take a little more time to focus on your prayer life and share the experience with friends.

The ideal is for a parish to take up *Rejoice!* and travel together as a community. You can learn more about how to provide *Rejoice!* to a large parish group at **rejoiceprogram.com.** You will also find information there about bulk discounts and parish mission nights with *Rejoice!* videos.

If you cannot experience *Rejoice!* as a parish, consider a small group setting. Use *Rejoice!* as a family devotion for Advent, or get together with friends to discuss how God is speaking to you during this season. Bulk pricing for small groups is available.

You might also want to use *Rejoice!* as an individual. You can take this journey through Advent even if you are not meeting in a group or talking about it with friends. You are not alone—Catholics all over the country are traveling with you. This journal is a place for praying and learning to hear God's voice.

Videos

To accompany the journal, *Rejoice!* offers videos with Fr. Mark Toups, Sr. Josephine Garrett, and Fr. Josh Johnson. Through their witness, conversation, and prayer, you will find fresh insights into the liturgical readings for Advent, Year B.

The program includes a primary *Rejoice!* video and weekly themed videos. Each Sunday of Advent, you will get access to a quick video to energize your meditations and encourage you in your prayer that week. Sign up for these weekly videos at **rejoiceprogram.com** to receive them by email.

Daily Meditations

The Sunday readings for Advent, Year B, are included at the start of the week. Each day, a new meditation invites you to listen to God's voice as you journey to Christ's birth. The meditation begins with a word to orient your prayer and a brief passage from one of the readings. The day's meditation closes with a prompt titled "For Your Prayer" and lines for journaling to help you open your heart to the Lord.

The meditations for Sunday through Wednesday look back on the Sunday readings you heard at Mass, and the ones for Thursday through Saturday look forward to the upcoming Sunday readings.

The daily meditations shift to guided, imaginative prayers for the fourth week of Advent. Each meditation sets a scene and invites you to enter that scene personally as you pray.

The number of days in the last week of Advent varies from year to year, so you'll find seven daily meditations to cover them all. The last guided meditation is for Christmas Day.

Weekly Reflections and Discussion Questions

At the end of each week, we invite you to go back over the week's meditations and journal about your experience. We include three questions at the end of each Saturday meditation to help with this. Many people will find it fruitful to discuss the questions when they meet with others in their parish or small group, or you can ponder them on your own. The prayer shared in the video is included at the end of each week so you can easily read it and pray along with the presenters. Use them to reflect on your experience through the week—with the video presentation, the daily meditations, and your journal entries. Notice how your prayer might be changing, and write about the things that have touched you most deeply during the week.

Approaching Prayer

As you dedicate yourself to prayer this Advent, there is no better safeguard than a good plan. Fr. Josh Johnson, one of the presenters in the *Rejoice!* videos, recommends using the five Ws to make a plan. Here's how they work: Every Sunday, look at your calendar and write out your plan for the next six days. Make the plan specific by answering the five W questions—When? Where? What? Who? and Why?

When will I spend time with Jesus?

Where will I spend time with Jesus?

What are Jesus and I going to do together?

Who will hold me accountable for my time with Jesus?

Why am I prioritizing my time with Jesus?

With your plan in place, you may find these steps helpful when praying with Scripture and other texts:

Prepare

Read the text once to get familiar with the words. If you are praying imaginatively, read through the whole scene. Then slowly read the text a second time. Pay attention to how you feel as you read. Notice which words strike you. If the text sets a scene, enter it with the people mentioned. Imagine the scene in as much detail as possible.

Sometimes it helps to read the passage a third time. Enter it fully, and linger with it until it feels right to move on.

Acknowledge

You have read the text. You have entered the scene. Now *acknowledge* what stirs within you. Pay attention to your thoughts, feelings, and desires. They are important.

Relate

When you have acknowledged what is going on inside your heart, *relate* that to God. Don't just think about your thoughts, feelings, and desires. Don't just think about God or how God might react. Relate to God. Tell him how you feel. Tell him what you think. Tell him what you want. Share all your thoughts, feelings, and desires with him.

Receive

When you have shared everything with God, it's time to *receive* from him. Listen to what he is telling you. It could be a subtle voice you hear. It could be a memory that pops up. Maybe he invites you to reread the Scripture passage. Maybe he invites you into a still, restful silence. Trust that God is listening to you, and receive what he wants to share with you. Stay here as long as you desire.

Respond

Now *respond*. Your response could be continuing your conversation with God or resolving to do something. It could be tears or laughter. Respond to what you are receiving.

Journal

The last step is to journal. Keep a record of what your prayer is like. Your journal entry does not have to be lengthy. It can be a single word or sentence about what God told you or how the day's meditation struck you. However you do it, journaling will help you walk closer with God this Advent. We have provided space for you here to journal every day and at the end of every week.

Commit

Advent can be a busy season. Making a commitment is the first step in transforming your prayer life. These weeks with *Rejoice! An Advent Pilgrimage into the Heart of Scripture, Year B* are the perfect time to begin.

The First Week of Advent

Hear

First Reading

Isaiah 53:16B–17, 19B; 64:2–7

You, LORD, are our father,
  our redeemer you are named forever.
Why do you let us wander, O LORD, from your ways,
  and harden our hearts so that we fear you not?
Return for the sake of your servants,
  the tribes of your heritage.

Oh, that you would rend the heavens and come down,
  with the mountains quaking before you,
while you wrought awesome deeds we could not hope for,
  such as they had not heard of from of old.
No ear has ever heard, no eye ever seen, any God but you
  doing such deeds for those who wait for him.

Would that you might meet us doing right,
  that we were mindful of you in our ways!

Behold, you are angry, and we are sinful;
  all of us have become like unclean people,
  all our good deeds are like polluted rags;
we have all withered like leaves,
  and our guilt carries us away like the wind.
There is none who calls upon your name,
  who rouses himself to cling to you;
for you have hidden your face from us
  and have delivered us up to our guilt.

Yet, O LORD, you are our father;
  we are the clay and you the potter:
  we are all the work of your hands.

Responsorial Psalm

Psalm 80:2-3, 15-16, 18-19

R. Lord, make us turn to you; let us see your face and we shall be saved.

O shepherd of Israel, hearken,
    from your throne upon the cherubim, shine forth.
Rouse your power,
    and come to save us.

Once again, O LORD of hosts,
    look down from heaven, and see;
take care of this vine,
    and protect what your right hand has planted,
    the son of man whom you yourself made strong.

May your help be with the man of your right hand,
    with the son of man whom you yourself made strong.
Then we will no more withdraw from you;
    give us new life, and we will call upon your name.

Second Reading

1 Corinthians 1:3-9

Brothers and sisters: Grace to you and peace from God our Father and the Lord Jesus Christ.

I give thanks to my God always on your account for the grace of God bestowed on you in Christ Jesus, that in him you were enriched in every way, with all discourse and all knowledge, as the testimony to Christ was confirmed among you, so that you are not lacking in any spiritual gift as you wait for the revelation of our Lord Jesus Christ.

He will keep you firm to the end, irreproachable on the day of our Lord Jesus Christ. God is faithful, and by him you were called to fellowship with his Son, Jesus Christ our Lord.

Gospel

Mark 13:33-37

Jesus said to his disciples: "Be watchful! Be alert! You do not know when the time will come.

"It is like a man traveling abroad. He leaves home and places his servants in charge, each with his own work, and orders the gatekeeper to be on the watch. Watch, therefore; you do not know when the Lord of the house is coming, whether in the evening, or at midnight, or at cockcrow, or in the morning. May he not come suddenly and find you sleeping. What I say to you, I say to all: 'Watch!'"

BEFORE

"Lord, make us turn to

you; let us see your face

and we shall be saved."

—Psalm Response for the
First Sunday of Advent

WELCOME TO ADVENT.

Welcome to this sacred journey through the Sunday readings for Advent. As we begin the journey together, I assume many of you have been here before. Welcome back! And if this is your first experience with *Rejoice!*, I extend a special welcome. It is a profound privilege to embark on this journey with you.

Many of us have been welcomed here before. Most of us are familiar with Advent, and many of us are familiar with the gift of *Rejoice!* I, too, have been here before. This book marks my sixth in the *Rejoice!* series. Each year as we begin, we do so with familiar words in familiar surroundings. The question for us today is not "Where are we?" but "Why are we here?" Why Advent? Why *Rejoice?*

Advent cannot be fully understood in and of itself. Advent must be understood in its connection to Christmas. Advent leads us somewhere or, to be more specific, to someone.

Why are we here? We are here because God is not invisible. He is not remote. We are here because God wants to be known. He longs for us to have a relationship with him and sent us his Son, Jesus, to reveal himself to us. In Jesus, God has a heart to love us, hands to embrace us, and ears to listen to us. And yes, in Jesus, God has a face. In Jesus, God can be seen. He is not invisible.

Listen to the response in the Responsorial Psalm for the First Sunday of Advent, which is based on a line from Psalm 80: "Lord, make us turn to you; let us see your face and we shall be saved." I love this verse. We are asking God for help: "Lord, make us turn to you." In a sense, we are saying, "God, there is so much going on in my life, so much going on at this time of year. I can't find you easily, so please help me turn to you."

The response goes on to say, "Let us see your face." Imagine for a moment what it would be like for you if, at the end of this Advent journey, you could actually experience in your heart what it would be like to see the face of God. Imagine for a moment: What else do you desire more than to see the face of God? Isn't this the ache and yearning of the human heart? Isn't this the longing of every soul?

Why are we here? Because everyone desires to see the face of God. That gift, given to us at Christmas, starts today as we begin the Advent journey.

So yes, many of us have been here before. But you are different. This year is unique. As you are now, you have never been here this year, with this *Rejoice!*, as this unique Advent awaits you. Therefore, let's begin today as we have begun before. Ask the Lord to help you to be present to him in the moment. Ask for all you desire. Ask for the grace to see his face.

For Your Prayer

Pray with the Responsorial Psalm from the Sunday readings (Psalm 80:2–3, 15–16, 18–19). Read the verses three times and see if a word or phrase tugs at your heart.

**What words stood out to you as you prayed?
What did you find stirring in your heart?**

_____

_____

_____

_____

_____

_____

_____

_____

_____

_____

_____

_____

_____

_____

_____

_____

_____

_____

First Week — SUNDAY

EXPECTATIONS

"Yet, O LORD, you are our Father;
we are the clay, and
you are our potter:
we are all the work of your hand."*

—Isaiah 64:8

---

* The Scripture passages quoted in the daily meditations are taken from the
Revised Standard Version–Second Catholic Edition. Their wording differs from
that of the Sunday readings, which are taken from the *Lectionary for Mass*, but
the translations complement each other and shed light on the passages when
read together.

YESTERDAY WAS THE SABBATH.

At Mass on the First Sunday of Advent, in the first reading from the prophet Isaiah, we heard words like these: "Yet, O LORD, you are our Father; we are the clay, and you are our potter; we are all the work of your hand" (Isaiah 64:8).

On the one hand, I find those words deeply consoling. Imagine the inner freedom we would all enjoy if life were as easy as being the clay in the hands of God, "the potter." Imagine what our lives, marriages, and families would look like if the Almighty himself were directing every thought and action in our lives. Imagine what our communities, nation, world, and Church would look like with that foretaste of heaven.

Imagine that. When I do, I am filled with hope.

Yet on the other hand, despite my hope and desire, I know too well that instead of living as the work of his hand, my real work is trying not to fight the potter. Sometimes I want to be the potter; I don't want to be merely the clay. This is the battle of the spiritual life: between God and me, between control and surrender.

We experience this tension clearly in the battle between expectations and desire. Desire is good. Desire is from God. In fact, God *is* desire. He made us; we exist only because we are desired. We are not *needed* by God; we are *desired* by God. The fact that each of us has desires for God is because God himself placed those desires in us. It is healthy for us to name our desires. We need to relate those desires to the Lord. When we do so, God can respond as God desires. God can bring our desires to their natural fulfillment.

Expectations differ from desires not in substance but in fulfillment. Let me explain. Expectations are our desires cloaked in control. When we have expectations, we attempt to control how and when our desires will be fulfilled. Expectations limit God and, inevitably, far too often disappoint us.

With that said, I invite you to surrender your expectations of what this Advent will look like. As I said yesterday, you are different this Advent. This year is unique. You have never been here as you are now, with this *Rejoice!*, as this unique Advent awaits you. This year's *Rejoice!* is inviting you to experience Advent in a whole new way as you learn to hear God's voice.

While naming your desires, let go of your expectations. Let the Lord do what he wants, and trust that he will do far more than you could ever ask or imagine.

For Your Prayer

The psalms are at the heart of Jewish spirituality. Mary and Joseph would have prayed them daily. Today pray Psalm 63. As you read it, imagine Mary and Joseph reciting the same words as they prayed during that first Advent. Read it three times and see if a word or phrase tugs at your heart.

What words stood out to you as you prayed? What did you find stirring in your heart?

_____

_____

_____

_____

_____

_____

_____

_____

_____

_____

_____

_____

_____

_____

_____

_____

_____

_____

_____

_____

First Week — MONDAY

PSALMS

66 Give us life, and
we will call on
your name! **99**

—Psalm 80:18

I INVITE YOU TO JOIN

me today as we travel back in time. Imagine for a moment that you can go back to that very first Advent. Imagine that you can go back two thousand years to actually be with Mary and Joseph as they prepare for the birth of Jesus. What do they feel? What is their relationship like? How do they get ready? I have long been fascinated with the humanity of Mary and Joseph. What I would give to be back there with them at that very moment!

In this moment, let us imagine Mary. She is eight months pregnant, with merely four weeks until the birth of her son. We can see her now, caressing her belly as she sings to her son within. We can imagine Joseph as strong yet contemplative. He is here with his wife, attentive to her needs. As he works rhythmically through his day, he hums a sweet melody familiar to them both.

Let us imagine what they were like. What is Mary singing? What is Joseph thinking about as he works?

The psalms express the deepest longings of the human heart and God's unwearied pursuit of man. They touch on every human emotion and every ordinary situation. The psalms are the Bible's poetic prose, meant to be sung to praise the King of kings. The psalms were the canvas on which ancient Jewish families painted their love for the Lord. Devout Jews sang the psalms from memory at the synagogue and at home.

If you ever wonder how Mary prayed, you need to look no further than the psalms. If you ever wonder what words Joseph uttered to the Lord, look no further than the psalms. For a moment, let us imagine Mary resting in their home in Nazareth, with her hands gently clasped on her pregnant belly as she sings from Psalm 22:

"Upon you was I cast from my birth, and since my mother bore me, you have been my God." Let us imagine Joseph beholding Mary with great affection from across the room as he sings from Psalm 127: "Behold, sons are a heritage from the LORD, the fruit of the womb a reward."

I invite you to join me this Advent as we travel back in time. The psalms and other Scripture passages will help us on our way. Whenever you pray with a psalm or another passage from the Old Testament, you will be uttering the same sacred words that were familiar to Mary and Joseph in that first Advent. Let their words, especially the words of the psalms, be your prayer.

For Your Prayer

Today pray with Psalm 37:1–7. As you read it, imagine Mary and Joseph reciting the same words during that first Advent. Read it three times and see if a word or phrase tugs at your heart.

What words stood out to you as you prayed?
What did you find stirring in your heart?

_____

_____

_____

_____

_____

_____

_____

_____

_____

_____

_____

_____

_____

_____

_____

_____

_____

_____

_____

_____

_____

INITIATIVE

" Stir up your might, and

come to save us! ...

Turn again, O God of hosts! "

Look down from heaven, and see;

have regard for this vine.

—Psalm 80:2, 14

WITH TODAY'S MEDITATION,

we wrap up a few preliminary encouragements for this Advent. I want to look specifically at God's tireless initiative, which can have a transformative influence on our prayer during this Advent season and beyond.

There is an old Catholic saying that grace builds on nature. This means that we can learn a lot about our spiritual lives if we pay attention to the world in which we live. For example, this time of year has many of us preparing for holiday celebrations. Life is busier from Thanksgiving to Christmas than at any other time. There are lists to be made and things to be done. Our minds are filled with a litany of all the tasks we are responsible for.

Underneath the busyness of the holiday season are two things that drive our activity: our initiative and self-responsibility. The busier we are, the more we feel responsible for completing the tasks on our to-do list. This interior posture may help us stay on track in the holiday frenzy, but it can harm our prayer and our relationship with God.

Let's pay attention to the theological reality of the Incarnation. If we do that, we see clearly that God is forever taking the initiative. God is the one who promised through prophecy in the Old Testament that he would send the Messiah. God is the one who sent the Angel Gabriel to Mary. God is the one who conceived life in the womb of the Virgin. God is the one who took the initiative to become man and reveal himself to us in the flesh. Our God is a God who is forever taking the initiative. He is ceaselessly reaching out to us.

Furthermore, because he takes the initiative in our lives, God wants the responsibility of leading us. When you and I feel the burden of responsibility, it threatens our capacity for receptivity. Prayer becomes just another item on our to-do list, another task to complete and check off. Instead of receiving from God, we may be tempted to make things happen. But on our own initiative, we cannot lure God to us. We cannot produce spiritual experiences under our own power.

But this does not need to be the case, nor is it God's desire for us. Remember: God is forever taking the initiative. He wants us to rest this Advent as he leads us through the meditations, the season, and our preparations for Christmas.

Relax. Take a deep breath. Let the Lord take the lead. Let the Lord take responsibility.

For Your Prayer

Today pray Psalm 37:1–7 again, as you did yesterday. Imagine Mary and Joseph reciting the same words as they prayed during that first Advent. Read it three times and see if a word or phrase tugs at your heart.

What words stood out to you as you prayed?
What did you find stirring in your heart?

_____

_____

_____

_____

_____

_____

_____

_____

_____

_____

_____

_____

_____

_____

_____

_____

_____

_____

_____

_____

_____

_____

HEAR

" Let me hear what
God the LORD
will speak. **"**

—**Psalm 85:8**

AS I MENTIONED BEFORE,

the psalms are at the heart of Jewish spirituality. They are the canvas on which ancient Jewish families painted their love for the Lord.

One of the psalms that speak to me awaits us in the readings for the Second Sunday of Advent. In the first stanza of Psalm 85 we read, "Let me hear what God the LORD will speak" (Psalm 85:8).

There are three words and phrases in this verse for us to unpack: *hear*, *God the Lord*, and *speak*. First, it truly is possible for us to hear God's voice. You *can* hear God. Second, when we consider hearing God, it is good to remember who is speaking—namely, God the Lord. Third, God himself longs to speak to us.

Today let us unpack the word *hear*.

Yesterday we were reminded that God is forever taking the initiative in our lives. Keeping that in mind, we see in this verse that God *wants* to speak to us. God is taking the initiative in speaking to us. God wants to speak, and this means God wants us to hear. We were created by God, for God. When God made us, he made us so we could hear his voice. In addition, God uses everything possible to help us hear. For example, in the *Rite of Baptism for One Child,* the celebrant touches the ears and mouth of the child with his thumb, saying, "The Lord Jesus made the deaf hear and the dumb speak. May he soon touch your ears to receive his word, and your mouth to proclaim his faith, to the praise and glory of God the Father."

God *wants* us to hear.

Imagine what your life would look like if you could actually hear God. Imagine your relationship with him if you heard his voice more regularly. Imagine how confident you would be in knowing the direction of your life because you knew his voice was leading. The mere fact that you are reading a book like this indicates that you long for more in your relationship with God. You do want to hear him, don't you?

For most of us, it's not the longing that's the problem; it's the struggle. Many of us don't hear God. Maybe we've tried, and maybe we've asked before, or maybe we just struggle with distractions. Our experience may lie, suggesting that others are able to hear God but we can't.

Listen to me: I want you to ask. Your personal history and experience don't change God's desire to speak to you. I want you to ask. Today and every day during this Advent, I want you to ask God to help you hear his voice. In fact, don't just ask—beg. Beg God as if you were begging for breath.

For Your Prayer

Today read Jeremiah 29:11–14. Imagine Mary and Joseph praying these very words. Read the passage slowly three times. Ask God to reveal the word or phrase he is using to speak to you. What is God saying to you in the text?

What words stood out to you as you prayed?
What did you find stirring in your heart?

WHO

> "Let me hear what God
> the LORD will speak."
>
> —Psalm 85:8

TODAY WE CONTINUE

unpacking Psalm 85:8. Yesterday, I mentioned that there are three words and phrases we will look at in this verse: *hear*, *God the Lord*, and *speak*.

Yesterday we understood that it truly is possible for us to hear God's voice. *You* can hear God. Today let us unpack the phrase *God the Lord*.

The great Advent story consists of unique individual stories about those who were preparing for the birth of the Messiah during the very first Advent. In Luke 1, we read the story of Zechariah, the father of John the Baptist. Zechariah was a well-respected priest from the sons of Aaron who served in the great Temple in Jerusalem. We read, "It fell to him by lot to enter the temple of the Lord and burn incense. ... And there appeared to him an angel of the Lord standing on the right side of the altar of incense. And Zechariah was troubled when he saw him, and fear fell upon him. But the angel said to him, 'Do not be afraid, Zechariah, for your prayer is heard, and your wife Elizabeth will bear you a son, and you shall call his name John'" (Luke 1:9–13).

Zechariah heard God speak to him through the angel. But Zechariah doubted what he heard. The angel responded, "I am Gabriel, who stand in the presence of God, and I was sent to speak to you, and to bring you this good news. And behold, you will be silent and unable to speak until the day that these things come to pass because you did not believe my words" (Luke 1:19–20).

Zechariah doubted what he heard because he forgot to whom he was listening. I have done the same. I remember once when

I was ruminating about all my problems. After flippantly expressing my doubts to God, I heard him reply, "Who are you talking to?"

As we consider hearing God, let us be reminded who is speaking to us. He is *God the Lord*. He is more powerful than your doubts, distractions, or history of hearing him. He who holds all creation in existence on the tip of his finger at the same time takes the initiative to speak to you. Do not forget who he is.

Again, I want you to ask God to help you hear. Ask him to help, and trust that he will act.

For Your Prayer

Today read Psalm 85. Imagine how often Mary, Joseph, and Zechariah would have prayed these very words. Read the passage slowly three times. Ask God to reveal the word or phrase he is using to speak to you. What is God saying to you in the text?

What words stood out to you as you prayed?
What did you find stirring in your heart?

_____

_____

_____

_____

_____

_____

_____

_____

_____

_____

_____

_____

_____

_____

_____

_____

_____

_____

_____

_____

_____

_____

_____

SPEAK

"Let me hear what God the
Lord will speak."

—Psalm 85:8

LET US TURN AGAIN

to Psalm 85:8: "Let me hear what God the LORD will speak." On Thursday I mentioned that we will unpack three words or phrases: *hear*, *God the Lord*, and *speak*. We have seen that we can hear God's voice. *You* can hear God. And we have seen that it is good to remember who is speaking to us, namely, God the Lord.

Today let us unpack the word *speak*, for God longs to speak to us.

How does God speak to us? How do we actually hear God? I used to think that God's voice sounded like the voice of James Earl Jones. (I love his voice!) I was expecting a big, booming voice within me that would be unmistakably God's voice. But this is not how God speaks to me.

Let's start with his Word. God has already spoken in his Word, in the Bible. Every one of the words in the Bible can be trusted as absolutely inspired by God. God speaks to us when we read the Bible. God also may speak to us through a thought that "sounds" like the other thoughts in our heads but has a different source. If I pay attention to my interior life, I discover that some thoughts occur because I am "driving" them. For example, when I woke up this morning, my first thoughts were that I needed to make coffee and prepare for the day. Those thoughts happened because I drove them. I was the source of those thoughts.

Other thoughts simply come to me without my initiative. Sometimes when I pray, a thought simply comes to me. Such thoughts sound like the other thoughts in my head, but what's different is that I'm not driving them. These thoughts just gently come to me.

God can also speak to us through a physiological sensation in our body, such as warmth in our chest or a sense of peace. God can speak to us through a memory that pops up or a song that instantly comes to mind. And sometimes God speaks to us through others, assuming that others are docile enough to let God use them.

God not only wants to speak to us, but he is actively speaking to us now. Perhaps the grace is not in hoping that God *will* speak but in learning more about how he actually *is* speaking. Again, I want you to ask God to help you hear. Ask him to help, and trust that he will act.

For Your Prayer

Today read the Scripture readings for the Second Sunday of Advent on pages 40–43. Reading them now will better prepare you to hear God speak to you at Mass. Ask the Lord to reveal the words of the text that he is using to speak to you about your life.

What words stood out to you as you prayed?
What did you find stirring in your heart?

_____

_____

_____

_____

_____

_____

_____

_____

_____

_____

_____

_____

_____

_____

_____

_____

_____

_____

_____

_____

First Week — SATURDAY

Here are three questions to help you reflect on this week's meditations. You may find it helpful to discuss them with others or ponder them on your own before you begin the weekly reflection:

- How does your heart react to the verse "we are the clay, and you are our potter"? Is it comforting or troubling to recognize that God is in control? What are some ways you can surrender to his will?

- How do you best hear the voice of God? Can you recall a time you heard his voice speaking to your heart?

- **VIDEO REFLECTION:** What is the experience of silence like for you? Do you ever encounter silence? If you do, how does it make you feel?

Now take a moment to reflect on the past week, going over the meditations that bore the most fruit in your prayer, the things you wrote, and your reflections on this week's video. How has your prayer changed this week?

_____

_____

_____

_____

_____

_____

_____

_____

_____

_____

ON SILENCE

"Technical progress, especially in the area of transport and communications, has made human life more comfortable but also more keyed up, at times even frenetic. … Unbeknownst to them, people are increasingly becoming immersed in a virtual dimension because of the audiovisual messages that accompany their life from morning to night. The youngest … seem to want to fill every empty moment with music and images, out of fear of feeling this very emptiness. This is a trend that has always existed, … but today it has reached a level such as to give rise to talk about anthropological mutation. Some people are no longer able to remain for long periods in silence and solitude."

—Pope Benedict XVI, Homily (October 9, 2011)

The Second Week of Advent

Speak

First Reading

Isaiah 40:1–5, 9–11

Comfort, give comfort to my people,
    says your God.
Speak tenderly to Jerusalem, and proclaim to her
    that her service is at an end,
    her guilt is expiated;
indeed, she has received from the hand of the Lord
    double for all her sins.

A voice cries out:
In the desert prepare the way of the Lord!
    Make straight in the wasteland a highway for our God!
Every valley shall be filled in,
    every mountain and hill shall be made low;
the rugged land shall be made a plain,
    the rough country, a broad valley.
Then the glory of the Lord shall be revealed,
    and all people shall see it together;
    for the mouth of the Lord has spoken.

Go up on to a high mountain,
    Zion, herald of glad tidings;
cry out at the top of your voice,
    Jerusalem, herald of good news!
Fear not to cry out
    and say to the cities of Judah:
    Here is your God!

Here comes with power
  the Lord GOD,
   who rules by his strong arm;
here is his reward with him,
   his recompense before him.
Like a shepherd he feeds his flock;
   in his arms he gathers the lambs,
carrying them in his bosom,
   and leading the ewes with care.

Responsorial Psalm

Psalm 85:9–10, 11–12, 13–14

*R. Lord, let us see your kindness, and grant us
your salvation.*

I will hear what God proclaims;
   the LORD—for he proclaims peace to his people.
Near indeed is his salvation to those who fear him,
   glory dwelling in our land.

Kindness and truth shall meet;
   justice and peace shall kiss.
Truth shall spring out of the earth,
   and justice shall look down from heaven.

The LORD himself will give his benefits;
   our land shall yield its increase.
Justice shall walk before him,
   and prepare the way of his steps.

Second Reading

2 Peter 3:8–14

Do not ignore this one fact, beloved, that with the Lord one day is like a thousand years and a thousand years like one day. The Lord does not delay his promise, as some regard "delay," but he is patient with you, not wishing that any should perish but that all should come to repentance.

But the day of the Lord will come like a thief, and then the heavens will pass away with a mighty roar and the elements will be dissolved by fire, and the earth and everything done on it will be found out.

Since everything is to be dissolved in this way, what sort of persons ought you to be, conducting yourselves in holiness and devotion, waiting for and hastening the coming of the day of God, because of which the heavens will be dissolved in flames and the elements melted by fire. But according to his promise we await new heavens and a new earth in which righteousness dwells.

Therefore, beloved, since you await these things, be eager to be found without spot or blemish before him, at peace.

Gospel

Mark 1:1-8

The beginning of the gospel of Jesus Christ the Son of God.

As it is written in Isaiah the prophet: *Behold, I am sending my messenger ahead of you; he will prepare your way. A voice of one crying out in the desert: "Prepare the way of the Lord, make straight his paths."*

John the Baptist appeared in the desert proclaiming a baptism of repentance for the forgiveness of sins. People of the whole Judean countryside and all the inhabitants of Jerusalem were going out to him and were being baptized by him in the Jordan River as they acknowledged their sins.

John was clothed in camel's hair, with a leather belt around his waist. He fed on locusts and wild honey.

And this is what he proclaimed: "One mightier than I is coming after me. I am not worthy to stoop and loosen the thongs of his sandals. I have baptized you with water; he will baptize you with the Holy Spirit."

BEST

"He will speak peace

to his people."

—Psalm 85:8

AS WE LEARN MORE

about how to hear God's voice, I would like to bring you back to where we were on Friday when I talked about the importance of remembering who is speaking. It is the Lord, and he is so very, very good. God always and only wants what is best for us. God always desires to "speak peace to his people" (Psalm 85:8).

The Hebrew word translated "peace" in Psalm 85:8 is *shalom*. In ancient Judaism, *shalom* meant more than simple peace, lack of conflict, or good tidings. *Shalom* referred to safety, welfare, health, prosperity, quiet, tranquility, contentment, and friendship. All these are attributes of the peace that God speaks to his people. In essence, when God speaks peace to his people, he expresses his desire for your good. God desires only what is best for us. He not only knows what is best for us, but he desires it.

When hearing God, we must remember that he is the Lord and that he wants only what is best for us. Since we are on this Advent journey, let me share two examples from Mary and Joseph's life.

In the Gospel of Luke, we read of Mary's Annunciation. God sends the angel Gabriel to Mary with the message of the Incarnation. The virginal conception of Jesus requires Mary to trust in God. Scripture says that "she was greatly troubled" during the Annunciation (Luke 1:29). While she trusts that God will do what the angel says, she is confused about how it will happen. The angel speaks directly to Mary's question when he says, "Do not be afraid" (Luke 1:30).

In the Gospel of Matthew, we read of Joseph's annunciation. Joseph understands that Mary is with child, and he is troubled. The news requires him to trust in God. His heart is filled with emotions, and his mind is racing with questions. Then the angel appears to Joseph in a dream with words of reassurance. God sends the angel to Joseph to say, "Do not fear" (Matthew 1:20).

Neither Mary nor Joseph expected to hear the news they received from God. Both of them were called to trust. Specifically, they had to trust that God wanted only what was best for them. While the Incarnation was not in their plans, Mary and Joseph trusted *who* spoke to them as much as they trusted *what* was said.

The same is true for you. You can always trust God: *always*. You can trust him because of who he is and because he wants only what is best for you.

For Your Prayer

Today read Psalm 37:1–7. Imagine how often Mary and Joseph would have prayed these very words. Read the passage slowly three times. Ask God to reveal the word or phrase he is using to speak to you. What is God saying to you in the text?

What words stood out to you as you prayed?
What did you find stirring in your heart?

TRUTH

"Mercy and faithfulness
will meet."

—Psalm 85:10

THE VERSES OF THE

psalm read on the Second Sunday of Advent are from Psalm 85. In Psalm 85:10 we read, "Mercy and faithfulness will meet." The Hebrew word translated as "faithfulness" is *emet*, which means "firmness, faithfulness, sureness, reliability, stability, continuance, and truth." Psalm 85 teaches us that when God speaks to us, he speaks only *emet*; he speaks only truth.

Let us return to what we may learn from Mary during Advent. During the Annunciation, the angel spoke to her on behalf of God, saying, "And behold, your kinswoman Elizabeth in her old age has also conceived a son; and this is the sixth month with her who was called barren. For with God nothing will be impossible" (Luke 1:36–37).

After the angel left, Luke tells us, "Mary arose and went with haste into the hill country, to a city of Judah" to visit Elizabeth, who was her cousin. The walk from Nazareth to the hill country of Judah would have taken a little less than a week. During that time, Mary knew that God's words were true, even though she lacked other evidence. Soon she "entered the house of Zechariah and greeted Elizabeth." Elizabeth exclaimed, "Blessed is she who believed that there would be a fulfilment of what was spoken to her from the Lord" (Luke 1:39, 40, 45).

When Mary greeted Elizabeth, she saw firsthand that Elizabeth was indeed pregnant. However, this evidence only confirmed what Mary *already* knew to be true. The truth of God's promise was not dependent on physical evidence. Mary knew whose voice she heard. Mary knew that God's words are always true. Thus, she knew that Elizabeth was indeed pregnant because she knew the one who said it.

There may be moments in your life when you hear God speak to you about something he will do in the future. Many times we have to wait for these words to come to fulfillment. In the waiting, we may be tempted to doubt whether God will come through on his promise. Because we don't see as God sees, we don't trust as he asks us to trust. In those moments, we are tempted to doubt what we've heard because we lack evidence that confirms God's words. In those moments, may we learn from Mary, who trusted God's words because she trusted God himself.

How is God is asking you to trust him? What particular people, circumstances, or prayers require your trust? Do not be afraid. Listen to God's voice. His words are always true.

For Your Prayer

Today read Psalm 91. Imagine how often Mary and Joseph would have prayed these very words. Read the passage slowly three times. Ask God to reveal the word or phrase he is using to speak to you. What is God saying to you in the text?

What words stood out to you as you prayed?
What did you find stirring in your heart?

SEE

"Righteousness will
go before him,
and make his
footsteps a way."

—Psalm 85:13

IN THESE FIRST DAYS

of our pilgrimage through Advent, a theme has emerged that will continue to unfold during our journey: God longs for you to hear his voice. I pray that this Advent will be a sacred time as you become more and more sensitive to hearing God's voice.

If we are to hear God, we may need to *see* him better, for our senses work together. We often don't hear as God desires because we don't see as God sees.

St. Ignatius of Loyola has long since been my favorite saint. He has influenced me more than any other saint by far. In his masterpiece, the Spiritual Exercises, Ignatius writes, "I will stand for the space of an Our Father, a step or two before the place where I am to meditate or contemplate, and with my consciousness raised on high, consider how my God and Lord beholds me. Then I will make an act of reverence or humility."*

Before Ignatius prays and seeks to hear God, he stops for sixty seconds to consider how God sees him. Why is this important? Far too often, I project onto God the disposition and nature of my interior state. If I am having a good day, I presume that God is excited to see me and is also having a good day. If I am having a bad day, I often erroneously presume that God is also having a bad day and may not have time to speak with me. Worse yet, if I am frustrated with myself, I project this onto God, and I presume God is also frustrated with me. I often project onto God how I see myself and presume that he sees me the same way. This has a significant influence on how receptive I am to hearing his voice.

---

* Ignatius, Spiritual Exercises, no. 75, as quoted in Philip Kosloski, "St. Ignatius' Powerful Advice on How to Begin Prayer," *Pope's Worldwide Prayer Network*, July 24, 2018, popesprayerusa.net.

Second Week — TUESDAY

The antidote for projection is intentionality. Ignatius, understanding the importance of knowing how God sees him, pauses for the space of an Our Father before he begins his prayer so that he can understand what God sees as God beholds him. He anchors himself in God's presence. This intentional spiritual exercise allows Ignatius to relax and be more docile. It makes him more sensitive to hearing God's voice.

I hope that you are spending as much time with the "For Your Prayer" prompts as you are with the meditations. In personal prayer, we will hear the Lord speak to us. Today be intentional about pausing for a minute before you actually pray. Ask the Lord to reveal what is in his heart and eyes as he beholds you.

For Your Prayer

Today read Isaiah 43:4. Imagine how often Mary and Joseph would have prayed these very words. Ask the Lord to show you what he sees when he sees you.

**What words stood out to you as you prayed?
What did you find stirring in your heart?**

_____

_____

_____

_____

_____

_____

_____

_____

_____

_____

_____

_____

_____

_____

_____

_____

_____

_____

_____

_____

_____

_____

Second Week — TUESDAY

SENSITIZED

" Let me hear what God
the LORD will speak. "

—Psalm 85:8

AS I MENTIONED

yesterday, a theme has emerged that will continue to unfold during our journey: God longs for you to hear his voice. I pray that this Advent, God will re-sensitize your ears so you can hear his voice personally.

What does it mean to have God re-sensitize our ears? Perhaps a story can help us. I love to fish. I fish almost once a week during the offseason and sometimes several times a week during the peak season of summer and fall. Most of my inland fishing for speckled trout and redfish is done in what South Louisiana calls "the marsh." Most of the coast of Cajun country is not pristine beaches but slowly eroding grassland, which is a magnificent habitat for fishing.

I arrive in the marsh early in the morning. If I am lucky enough to have no cell phone coverage and disciplined enough not to fill the quiet with noise, I am soon enveloped in silence. As the day continues, I grow more attuned to my surroundings. By midafternoon, I am astounded by how loud the marsh is: the chirping of crickets, the flutter of fish hunting at the water's edge, the call of birds. All these sounds were present at the day's beginning, but it took the day's silence to sensitize my ears to hear what was always there.

Many of us struggle to hear the voice of God. This is not because God is not speaking. It is more because of the noise that permeates our lives. The more we are disciplined and intentional in removing distractions from our day, the more our hearts will grow sensitive to the subtle voice of God, which is always there.

Allow me to offer you a simple challenge. I challenge you to remove all notifications from your cell phone for the next three days. Remove *all* dings, pings, and audio notifications. Remove all visual notifications other than essential functions such as the telephone, text messages, and email. Then put your phone on "Do Not Disturb." See what it is like for three days to live without the constant distraction of your phone.

In addition, carve out fifteen minutes of your day to spend in complete silence. Put your phone in another room, and remove yourself from human and technological distractions. During that fifteen-minute window, use the spiritual exercise in the "For Your Prayer" section below. Each day, pay attention to how you feel at the end of the fifteen minutes and how you feel without the distraction of the notifications from your phone.

For Your Prayer

Today read Psalm 127. Imagine how often Mary and Joseph would have prayed these very words. Read the passage slowly three times. Ask God to reveal the words he is using to speak to you. What is God saying to you in the text?

What words stood out to you as you prayed?
What did you find stirring in your heart?

INTENTIONAL

"Rejoice always."

—1 Thessalonians 5:16

HOW DID YOU DO WITH

yesterday's challenge? Did you remove all the notifications from your cell phone? If not, why not? As a veteran spiritual director and someone who practices relentless self-reflection, I believe that the two most prevalent influences on our ability to hear God are the pace at which we live and the incessant stimuli that fill that fill our days. Most of us have an authentic desire to hear God. The struggle is that most of us don't exercise intentionality about doing the small things we need to do to hear him.

St. Paul's exhortation in 1 Thessalonians may feel overwhelming to us. He writes, "Rejoice always, pray constantly, give thanks in all circumstances" (1 Thessalonians 5:16–18). Whew. Anything else? We'll read this particular Scripture passage in just a few days on the Third Sunday of Advent.

How can we implement St. Paul's seemingly impossible invitation in the world where we live? Most scholars agree that Paul wrote this letter in the winter months of late AD 50 or early 51. Thessalonica was a commercial city in northern Greece, and the Christian church there was young, small, and vulnerable. Paul knew that the Christians there would soon be persecuted for their faith. He knew they would persevere only if they remained intentional.

In northern Greece in AD 50, one of the threats to a life of holiness was posed by the Roman and Jewish leaders who wished to stop the spread of the Gospel. Those threats may seem irrelevant to us in the twenty-first century, but other threats to our holiness require attention and discernment. The essential virtue we need today is the same virtue the Christians of Thessalonica needed, namely, intentionality.

You and I are having this conversation in the month of December, which presents us with more challenges than the ordinary rhythm of the other eleven months does. But you and I are not alone in facing the challenges of remaining intentional.

Let us consider for a moment the extraordinary challenges that confronted Mary and Joseph in the very first Advent: the emotions surrounding the awesome task of being chosen to raise the Messiah, the physical exertion of their long pilgrimage to Bethlehem, and the difficulties of finding a shelter in Bethlehem where Mary could give birth to Jesus. All these things required them to remain intentional about listening to the voice of God.

Mary and Joseph had to remain intentional as do you and I. Therefore, let us continue today the exercise we began yesterday: Spend fifteen minutes of your day in complete silence. Put your phone in another room, and remove yourself from human and technological distractions. During those fifteen minutes, do the spiritual exercise in the "For Your Prayer" section below. Pay attention to how you feel at the end of the exercise and how you feel without the distraction of your phone.

For Your Prayer

Read the Scripture readings for the Third Sunday of Advent on pages 80–83. Reading them now will better prepare you to hear God speak to you at Mass. Ask the Lord to reveal the words of the text that he is using to speak to you about your life.

What words stood out to you as you prayed?
What did you find stirring in your heart?

_____

_____

_____

_____

_____

_____

_____

_____

_____

_____

_____

_____

_____

_____

_____

_____

_____

_____

_____

_____

Second Week — THURSDAY

AVAILABLE

> "My soul magnifies the Lord."
>
> —Luke 1:46

AS WE CONTINUE

to unpack the theme of hearing the Lord, we look ahead to the Scripture readings for the Third Sunday of Advent. The Responsorial Psalm is actually from Mary's *Magnificat*, the joyful words she spoke to Elizabeth at the Visitation. In these beautiful words we continue to learn how to hear the voice of the Lord.

In the Annunciation, we see that Mary hears God and trusts him fully. In the Visitation, we see a new dimension of her listening as she proclaims, "My soul magnifies the Lord" (Luke 1:46). How can Mary magnify God? How can a human being, who is of a lesser nature than God, magnify the omnipotent? Mary's soul is not greater than God, who created her. But because of the purity of Mary's heart, she is able to receive the spoken Word from God and magnify that Word with perfect reverberation and echo. Mary's heart is perfectly shaped to receive the Word of God, for she is completely available to God.

Mary is completely available. Nothing is off-limits. This complete availability allows her to hear God no matter what God wants to talk about.

If you and I are going to hear God, we too must ask for the grace to become more available to him, with nothing off-limits in our lives. Availability to God also means that we intentionally include God in every area of our life. Too often I make the mistake of limiting God to the mystical or religious areas of my life when God wants access to everyday life's practical and ordinary yet essential details.

Let me give you an example. For many of us at this time of year, many practical details occupy our minds—finishing our Christmas shopping, preparing for holiday gatherings, and anticipating how we celebrate Christmas. My question to you is this: How are your finances, and how are they affected by Christmas shopping? Do you have the necessary resources to get the gifts you've planned? Can you afford all the gifts your loved ones desire? With regard to the holiday gatherings, how are your relationships with the people who will be coming? Are there relationships that are strained and need to be mended? Is there someone who will attend whose presence brings anxiety? Is there a loved one who has passed away, whose absence elicits grief?

The Lord often wants to speak to us about these very practical details. When we are completely available to God in all areas of our life, we can hear him more as Mary did.

For Your Prayer

Today read the Scripture readings for the Third Sunday of Advent (pages 80–83) again. Reading them now will better prepare you to hear God speak to you at Mass. Ask the Lord to reveal the words of the text that he is using to speak to you about your life.

**What words stood out to you as you prayed?
What did you find stirring in your heart?**

_____

_____

_____

_____

_____

_____

_____

_____

_____

_____

_____

_____

_____

_____

_____

_____

_____

_____

_____

_____

_____

ATTUNED

"My spirit rejoices in
God my Savior."

—Luke 1:47

TODAY WE WILL LEARN

more from Mary about how she heard the voice of the Lord. In her *Magnificat*, Mary exclaims to Elizabeth, "My spirit rejoices in God my Savior" (Luke 1:47). Since Mary's heart is completely available to God, it makes sense that Mary rejoices in God. To rejoice is to take great joy or profound delight. To rejoice is to be fully open to the object of our affection. Mary rejoices in God because God is supremely important to her. It is the Lord who brings her joy. It is the Lord who fulfills the desires of her heart.

Mary's availability to God allows her heart to be in tune with God's voice. For Mary's heart to be attuned to the voice of God, Mary has to live in rhythm with God. When I consider what life must have been like in ancient Nazareth, I think the pace of Mary's life was different from the pace I have grown accustomed to. When I think about Mary living in Nazareth two thousand years ago, I don't imagine her caught up in a frenetic pace.

Too often, amid all our busyness, we feel as if we are not really living our lives. Rather, our lives are living us, driving us on at a frantic pace. The longer our to-do list, the faster the pace. This sense can be heightened in December, in these weeks before Christmas when there is so much to do.

I long to hear the voice of the Lord as Mary did. There seems to be a simple equation that illustrates Mary's ability to hear God's voice: availability + pace = attuned. For most of us, while availability is hard, accepting a slower, peaceful pace is even more challenging.

Pace is as much an interior disposition as it is an external action. For example, many of us find ourselves waiting more at this time of year. We wait in traffic, in lines at grocery stores, or within the sea of people at department stores. We can wait impatiently, interiorly rushing and interiorly fighting the wait. Or we can wait with surrender, interiorly praying without fighting the delay. Our disposition affects our pace.

There is also a direct relationship between external stimuli and how fast I move through the day. Whether it is music or nonstop conversation on the phone, any constant stimulus affects my sense of peace and makes it difficult to slow down.

It is impossible to imagine that Mary lived as fast as most of us do or with the many external stimuli most of us have. If we want to hear God's voice as Mary did, we must live a little bit more as she did. Let us begin today to attune our hearts to the Lord by reflecting on the pace at which we live.

For Your Prayer

Again, read the Scripture readings for the Third Sunday of Advent (pages 80–83). Reading them now will better prepare you to hear God speak to you at Mass. Ask the Lord to reveal the words of the text that he is using to speak to you about your life.

What words stood out to you as you prayed?
What did you find stirring in your heart?

_____

_____

_____

_____

_____

_____

_____

_____

_____

_____

_____

_____

_____

_____

_____

_____

_____

_____

_____

_____

_____

_____

Second Week — SATURDAY

Here are three questions to help you reflect on this week's meditations. You may find it helpful to discuss them with others or ponder them on your own before you begin the weekly reflection:

- Do you trust God? Do you believe he will come through for you? How is God asking you to trust him *now?*

- Did you take on the challenge of silencing nonessential notifications on your phone? If not, why? If you did, what did you notice?

- **VIDEO REFLECTION:** What line of the Litany of Letting Go in Prayer on the following pages convicted you the most? What emotions did it bring up in your heart?

Now take a moment to reflect on the past week, going over the meditations that bore the most fruit in your prayer, the things you wrote, and your reflections on this week's video. How has your prayer changed this week?

_____

_____

_____

_____

_____

_____

_____

_____

_____

_____

LITANY OF LETTING GO IN PRAYER

by Fr. Josh Johnson

Lord, have mercy. *Lord, have mercy.*
Christ, have mercy. *Christ, have mercy.*
Lord, have mercy. *Lord, have mercy.*

Jesus, help me to let go
of the belief that I am too busy to pray.

Jesus, help me to let go
of the belief that my work or ministry is more
important than prayer.

Jesus, help me to let go
of the belief that my prayer simply does not matter.

Jesus, help me to let go
of the belief that daily prayer is something only for
people I deem holier than myself.

Jesus, help me to let go
of the belief that I am not capable of waking up
earlier to make time for prayer.

Jesus, help me to let go
of the belief that I cannot silence my devices during
our time together in prayer.

Jesus, help me to let go
of the belief that if I get distracted, I will not be able
to return to you in prayer.

Jesus, help me to let go

  of the belief that I will offend my family or friends if I ask them to not disturb my time with you in prayer.

Jesus, help me to let go

  of the belief that something is wrong with my prayer if I'm not delighting in your presence or perceiving insights.

Jesus, help me to let go

  of the belief that I need to constantly examine my progress in the spiritual life while praying.

Jesus, help me to let go

  of the belief that I should dwell on my wounds instead of abiding in your Word.

Jesus, help me to let go

  of the belief that I can grow in my relationship with you apart from reading your Word in the Bible.

Jesus, help me to let go

  of the belief that I will never hear your voice when I pray.

Jesus, help me to let go

  of the belief that I will never experience your presence when I pray.

Jesus, help me to let go

  of the belief that I can control when and how you will communicate with me in prayer.

Jesus, help me to let go
> of the belief that silence in prayer is a
> negative experience.

Jesus, help me to let go
> of the belief that prayer is an optional practice.

Jesus, help me to let go
> of the belief that I can do anything apart from you.

Lord Jesus Christ, help me to remain faithful to my relationship with the Holy Trinity through the practice of daily prayer so that I may abide in relationship with you, our Father, and the Holy Spirit during my pilgrimage on earth and most importantly forever in the kingdom of heaven. Amen.

The Third Week of Advent

Heal

First Reading

Isaiah 61:1–2A, 10–11

The spirit of the Lord GOD is upon me,
because the LORD has anointed me;
he has sent me to bring glad tidings to the poor,
to heal the brokenhearted,
to proclaim liberty to the captives
and release to the prisoners,
to announce a year of favor from the LORD
and a day of vindication by our God.

I rejoice heartily in the LORD,
in my God is the joy of my soul;
for he has clothed me with a robe of salvation
and wrapped me in a mantle of justice,
like a bridegroom adorned with a diadem,
like a bride bedecked with her jewels.

As the earth brings forth its plants,
and a garden makes its growth spring up,
so will the Lord GOD make justice and praise
spring up before all the nations.

Responsorial Psalm

Luke 1:46–48, 49–50, 53–54

R. My soul rejoices in my God.

My soul proclaims the greatness of the Lord;
 my spirit rejoices in God my Savior,
for he has looked upon his lowly servant.
 From this day all generations will call me blessed.

The Almighty has done great things for me,
 and holy is his Name.
He has mercy on those who fear him
 in every generation.

He has filled the hungry with good things,
 and the rich he has sent away empty.
He has come to the help of his servant Israel
 for he has remembered his promise of mercy.

Second Reading

1 Thessalonians 5:16–24

Brothers and sisters: Rejoice always. Pray without ceasing. In all circumstances give thanks, for this is the will of God for you in Christ Jesus.

Do not quench the Spirit. Do not despise prophetic utterances. Test everything; retain what is good. Refrain from every kind of evil.

May the God of peace make you perfectly holy and may you entirely, spirit, soul, and body, be preserved blameless for the coming of our Lord Jesus Christ. The one who calls you is faithful, and he will also accomplish it.

Gospel

John 1:6-8, 19-28

A man named John was sent from God. He came for testimony, to testify to the light, so that all might believe through him. He was not the light, but came to testify to the light.

And this is the testimony of John. When the Jews from Jerusalem sent priests and Levites to him to ask him, "Who are you?" He admitted and did not deny it, but admitted, "I am not the Christ."

So they asked him, "What are you then? Are you Elijah?" And he said, "I am not." "Are you the Prophet?" He answered, "No."

So they said to him, "Who are you, so we can give an answer to those who sent us? What do you have to say for yourself?" He said: "I am *the voice of one crying out in the desert, make straight the way of the Lord,* as Isaiah the prophet said."

Some Pharisees were also sent. They asked him, "Why then do you baptize if you are not the Christ or Elijah or the Prophet?" John answered them, "I baptize with water; but there is one among you whom you do not recognize, the one who is coming after me, whose sandal strap I am not worthy to untie."

This happened in Bethany across the Jordan, where John was baptizing.

HUMILITY

"For he has regarded

the low estate of

his handmaiden."

—Luke 1:48

TODAY WE CONCLUDE

our reflections on Mary's heart and her ways of hearing the voice of the Lord. Mary says to Elizabeth that the Lord "has regarded the low estate of his handmaiden" (Luke 1:48). Handmaids were on the lowest tier of household servants, trained to respond to the slightest movement of their master's hands; they were to be "at hand" at a moment's notice. Mary names herself as the Lord's handmaiden, thus describing her humility and attentiveness to the slightest promptings of the Lord.

Mary's "low estate" also speaks to her humility. The humility that Mary describes is not a denial of all that is good within her. True humility is freedom from pride or arrogance. Mary knows who she is because she knows *whose* she is. She is completely available to God. She is the Lord's handmaiden. Mary belongs to the Lord. Thus, her true humility acknowledges God as the source of blessings.

Let us appreciate what humility looks like in our lives. Humility is not only thanking God for his blessings when they have been given; it also anchors us in depending on him as we ask him for blessings. Humility is not us operating on our own strength and then thanking God for a favorable outcome. True humility is acknowledging our absolute dependence on God in all things. This absolute dependence propels us to beg God from our interior poverty and then wait on him to guide us as he fulfills those desires.

In 2003, I made my first thirty-day silent retreat. It was a profound experience of learning how to pray at a deeper, more personal level. At the feet of a great spiritual director, I began to use the word *beg* when I asked the Lord for what I desired. I said, "Lord,

I beg you." The word *beg* elicits many things within us. To beg is to acknowledge our absolute dependence upon another to give us what we need. When I beg God, I'm not describing the intensity with which I want what I want; rather, I am acknowledging the intensity of my dependence upon God.

This type of humility, one that begs in acknowledgment of dependency, is a humility that disposes us to hear with a more attuned sensitivity. Mary's humility disposed her to hear God's voice as she did.

Humility, which begs in acknowledgment of dependency, is a gift God wants to give us. Today spend some time asking God for this gift. Be specific with your words. Ask God to help you understand what it means to beg and especially to beg him in complete dependence on him.

For Your Prayer

On page 155 of this book, you will find the Litany of Humility—a prayer that is both beautiful and, for many of us, challenging. Read it once to become familiar with the text. Then read it a second time more prayerfully, allowing the words to become your prayer.

What words stood out to you as you prayed?
What did you find stirring in your heart?

_____

_____

_____

_____

_____

_____

_____

_____

_____

_____

_____

_____

_____

_____

_____

_____

_____

_____

_____

_____

Third Week — SUNDAY

FAMILIAL

"Pray constantly."

—1 Thessalonians 5:17

TODAY WE BEGIN

to learn from Joseph how he heard the voice of the Lord. The second reading at Mass on the Third Sunday of Advent was from 1 Thessalonians, where St. Paul urges us to "pray constantly" (1 Thessalonians 5:17). While those words were not written to St. Joseph, they indeed would have described him.

In my book *Rejoice! Advent Meditations with Joseph* (Ascension, 2019), I included a few remarks on Matthew 1:19, where Joseph is described as "a just man." There, I quoted Pope Benedict XVI, who wrote, "The Old Testament idea of a whole life lived according to Sacred Scripture is summed up in the idea of 'a just man.'" The Holy Father continues: "Psalm 1 presents the classic image of the 'just' man. We might well think of it as a portrait of the spiritual figure of St. Joseph. A just man, it tells us, is one who maintains living contact with the word of God. ... He is like a tree planted beside the flowing waters. ... The flowing waters, from which he draws nourishment, naturally refer to the living word of God."*

Joseph's heart was attuned to the voice of God because his mind was attuned to the Word of God. To understand just how attuned Joseph was to the Word of God, perhaps we can appreciate the difference between the words *familiar* and *familial*. The word *familiar* means to have a well-known or close association with something or someone. One may use the word *familiar* to describe a close friendship, perhaps one of true intimacy.

The word *familial* relates to family bonds. The interesting thing about family bonds is that they cannot be existentially erased.

* Benedict XVI, *Jesus of Nazareth: The Infancy Narratives* (New York: Image, 2012), 39.

For example, I will always be the son of my parents and the brother of my siblings. This is a biological reality. Regardless of how close the affection or the relationship is, historically, I can never undo the fact that I am biologically in familial bonds with other people. Familial bonds run deeper than familiar bonds. The type of receptivity that Joseph had to the Word of God would be akin to the depth of a familial bond rather than simple familiarity. Joseph wasn't merely familiar with the Scriptures; he was as shaped by God's Word as one would be within his own family.

The more you and I spend time with the Word of God, the more you and I will become sensitized to the words of God. God has already spoken. If we want to hear God, then a natural place to start is with God's Word. The written words in the Bible are words that God uses to speak to us.

Let me offer you another challenge: For the next three days, set your alarm in three-hour increments—for example, at 9 a.m., 12 noon, 3 p.m., and 6 p.m. With each alarm, stop what you are doing and read a passage from Scripture for five minutes. Experiment with what it's like to reset the rhythm of your day with God's Word.

For Your Prayer

Today read Psalm 1. Imagine how often Mary and Joseph would have prayed these very words. Read the passage slowly three times. Ask God to reveal the word or phrase he is using to speak to you. What is God saying to you in the text?

What words stood out to you as you prayed?
What did you find stirring in your heart?

BALANCE

" Do not quench the Spirit. "

—1 Thessalonians 5:19

TODAY WE CONTINUE

to learn from Joseph how he heard the voice of the Lord. In the second reading at Mass on the Third Sunday of Advent, we heard, "Do not quench the Spirit" (1 Thessalonians 5:19). What are the things that quench the Spirit, and what does Joseph's interior life say to us about this?

While very little in the Bible explicitly speaks of St. Joseph, what is there speaks volumes about the man he was. In addition, the Tradition of the Church as a source of wisdom also tells us much. From these sources we know that God the Father needed an earthly vessel to reveal fatherhood to Jesus and image authentic masculinity. God hand-picked Joseph as an earthly father for Jesus, and thus Joseph was the ideal example and model.

As a husband and father, Joseph was a provider. Scripture tells us that he was a carpenter (Matthew 13:55), and as such he would have modeled for Jesus the balance between hard work and attention to family life. Thus, we can deduct from reason and implicit Scripture references that Joseph lived a life of balance.

Few things quench the Spirit more than a lack of balance in our lives. The temptation or burden of overwork, whether at work or home, can rob leisure. Leisure is necessary for re-creation. Re-creation is necessary for receptivity to the Lord. When we live balanced lives, we are more likely to experience joy and more likely to relax in prayer. When our interior state is at rest, we are sensitized to the subtle movements of God. Living well helps us hear well. Living a balanced life helps us hear God.

Living out of balance makes us susceptible to spiritual and physical fatigue. We are less present in the present moment.

Many of us have an interior opinion of why we live out of balance. For example, we may harbor resentment toward work or toward our responsibilities. We may judge ourselves because we are not often available to the people we love. These emotions and interior judgments can crowd our hearts and quench the interior state at rest.

If we want to hear well, we must live well. Let us begin by asking ourselves if we are living with balance. Here's my challenge to you today. Ask one or two people who know you best (such as your spouse, children, siblings, or close friends) if you are living life with balance. Ask them for concrete examples. Then talk to God about what you hear.

For Your Prayer

Today read Proverbs 17:22. Imagine how often Mary and Joseph would have prayed these very words. Read the passage slowly three times. Ask God to reveal the word or phrase he is using to speak to you. What is God saying to you in the text?

What words stood out to you as you prayed?
What did you find stirring in your heart?

_____

_____

_____

_____

_____

_____

_____

_____

_____

_____

_____

_____

_____

_____

_____

_____

_____

_____

_____

_____

_____

PRIORITIES

"
Test everything; hold
fast to what is good.
"

—1 Thessalonians 5:21

AS THE PASTOR OF A

small parish on an island vacation destination in South Louisiana, I have the privilege of having time available for alternative ministry in the winter months. My assignment allows me to receive priests on the island for spiritual direction, mentoring, and consultation. The island is an ideal setting for priests to get away from the pace of their parish. They often arrive in my office tired, scattered, or struggling. Recalling that grace builds on nature, I often begin my time with priests with fatherly words: "Go and get some sleep. Then take a long walk on the beach. Then we'll have a good meal together like ordinary human beings. Then, and only then, we can talk about what brought you here."

It always works, because grace does build on nature. Tending to the "human" things—such as adequate rest, healthy exercise, and a good meal—is necessary for the priest's receptivity to the "spiritual" things that brought him to the island. Our human reality influences our spiritual health. That's why the balance we talked about yesterday is so important.

Today we conclude our reflections on Joseph's heart and his ways of hearing the voice of the Lord. Joseph's life was balanced because the Lord properly ordered his priorities. Joseph's "human" reality influenced his "spiritual" health. Living with well-ordered priorities allowed Joseph to live a balanced life.

Nothing influences our sense of balance more than our priorities. A good friend once said, "Hope is not a strategy." Prayer—and living in a balanced way so that we can hear God's voice in the midst of it—most likely won't happen unless prayer and balance are priorities in our lives.

In the Second Reading at Mass on the Third Sunday of Advent, St. Paul admonishes us to "test everything; hold fast what is good" (1 Thessalonians 5:21). Test everything. This means discern everything. We must discern well what we consider important, what drives our decisions, and what we hold as priorities. To "hold fast what is good," we must recognize and acknowledge those things that compete with what is good in our lives.

When speaking of priorities, we should also remember that the enemy of the best is the good. In other words, we must often choose between two good things. The fact that something is good (work, provision, security, etc.) does not mean it is best or better (holiness, family, balance, etc.). Living well with the right priorities means that sometimes we must let go of something good to make room for the best.

For Your Prayer

Today read Deuteronomy 6:5 and Exodus 20:3. Imagine how often Mary and Joseph would have prayed these very words. Read the passage slowly three times. Ask God to reveal the word or phrase he is using to speak to you. What is God saying to you in the text?

What words stood out to you as you prayed?
What did you find stirring in your heart?

_____

_____

_____

_____

_____

_____

_____

_____

_____

_____

_____

_____

_____

_____

_____

_____

_____

_____

_____

_____

_____

_____

Third Week — WEDNESDAY

PATIENT

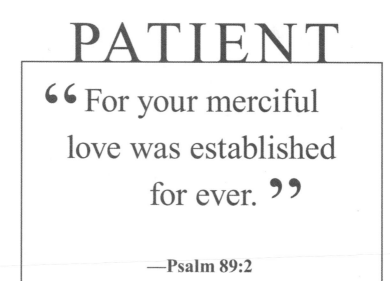

" For your merciful
love was established
for ever. "

—Psalm 89:2

IF WE ARE TO HEAR

the Lord, we must be patient. This coming Sunday, the Responsorial Psalm is Psalm 89, which is rich in mercy. In Psalm 89:2 we read, "For your merciful love was established forever." The psalm reminds us that God's love was established forever.

Forever. That is a long time. It's ... *forever.*

The forever love of God urges us to be patient. In fact, in his homily for the Twenty-Fifth World Day for Consecrated Life, Pope Francis said, "This is the reason for our hope: that God never tires of waiting for us. When we turn away, he comes looking for us; when we fall, he lifts us to our feet; when we return to him after losing our way, he waits for us with open arms. His love is not weighed in the balance of our human calculations but unstintingly gives us the courage to start anew. This teaches us resilience, the courage always to start each day again. Always to start over after our falls. God is patient."

Oh my, that makes my heart smile. God is patient. And if God is patient, we too need to be patient. The Holy Father continues:

There was a time when we responded to the Lord's call, and with enthusiasm and generosity offered our lives to him. Along the way, together with consolations, we have had our share of disappointments and frustrations. At times, our hard work fails to achieve the desired results, the seeds we sow seem not to bear sufficient fruit, the ardor of our prayer cools, and we are not always immune to spiritual aridity. ... It can happen that hope slowly fades as a result of unmet expectations. We must be patient with ourselves and await in hope God's own times and places, for he remains ever faithful to his promises. This is the foundation stone: he is true to his promises. Remembering this can help us retrace our steps and revive our dreams, rather than yielding to interior sadness and discouragement.*

That also makes my heart smile! Patience. God is patient, and we too must be patient. The Advent story teaches us about Mary's patience as she awaited the birth of her son. She had to be patient with Joseph as he surrendered to God's will. She had to be patient as they searched for a place in Bethlehem for her delivery. Mary teaches us that patience is a part of the spiritual life.

Joseph also teaches us about patience during Advent. Joseph had to be patient to hear God speak to him. He had to be patient with himself as he eventually surrendered to God's will. He had to be patient with the unexpected journey to his native homeland in Bethlehem.

If you and I are going to commit our lives to listening to God and hearing his voice, we must be people who are also committed to patience. Be patient with the process. Be patient with yourself. After all, God is patient with you. He will wait forever.

For Your Prayer

Read the Scripture readings for the Fourth Sunday of Advent on pages 118–121. Reading them now will better prepare you to hear God speak to you at Mass. Ask the Lord to reveal the words of the text that he is using to speak to you about your life.

---

* Francis, Homily (February 2, 2021), vatican.va.

**What words stood out to you as you prayed?
What did you find stirring in your heart?**

_____

_____

_____

_____

_____

_____

_____

_____

_____

_____

_____

_____

_____

_____

_____

_____

_____

_____

_____

_____

_____

_____

_____

Third Week — THURSDAY

MORE

"With my mouth
I will proclaim
your faithfulness to
all generations."

—Psalm 89:1

PSALM 89 HAS MUCH

to say to us about hearing God. In the first verse we read, "With my mouth I will proclaim your faithfulness to all generations." I love the psalms because they are the words Mary and Joseph would have used for their prayer in that first Advent and throughout their lives. I love the psalms because they are the words Mary and Joseph would have taught Jesus for his personal prayer. However, I love the psalms most of all because they express every human emotion, every longing, everything the human heart desires to share with God.

This weekend at Mass, we will proclaim and sing several verses from Psalm 89. Of all the things that our "mouths will proclaim," we are sure to acknowledge his "faithfulness to all generations." Alleluia.

God is faithful. God, whose voice we have longed to hear in our hearts this Advent, is faithful. Not only is he faithful, but he also wants to be heard infinitely more than we want to hear him. As much as we want God, he wants us more. As much as we want to hear him, he wants this more. When we proclaim his faithfulness, in a sense, we acknowledge that God desires us more.

I know no better news to proclaim than this: God became man because God longs for us to know him. God, who is forever taking the initiative, has spared no expense in revealing himself to us. He became man, he suffered and died on the Cross, he rose from the dead and ascended into heaven. What more could God do to impress on us this reality, that he wants us more than we want him? —

And the good news gets better. Nothing you and I have done or could do can diminish his desire for us. Indeed, sin affects our relationship with him—but not even sin extinguishes his desire for us. God is forever an unquenchable desire. Even with our personal shortcomings, spiritual inconsistencies, and times when we can't hear him, God longs for us. For that, we offer a great chorus of "Alleluia."

"With my mouth I will proclaim your faithfulness to all generations."

Our general teaching on hearing God is soon coming to a close. I encourage you to be patient (yesterday's meditation) and to ask for help (tomorrow's meditation). In the end, hearing God's voice hinges on his goodness, his fidelity, and the fact that he wants you to hear him even more than you do.

For Your Prayer

Read the Scripture readings for the Fourth Sunday of Advent on pages 118–121 again. Reading them now will better prepare you to hear God speak to you at Mass. Ask the Lord to reveal the words of the text that he is using to speak to you about your life.

What words stood out to you as you prayed?
What did you find stirring in your heart?

_____

_____

_____

_____

_____

_____

_____

_____

_____

_____

_____

_____

_____

_____

_____

_____

_____

_____

_____

_____

_____

_____

ASK

"My merciful love I will
keep for him for ever,
and my covenant will
stand firm for him."

—Psalm 89:28

TODAY WE CONTINUE

to unpack Psalm 89, which, as we have seen on Thursday and Friday, has much to say to us about hearing God. In verse 28 we read, "My merciful love I will keep for him forever, and my covenant will stand firm for him."

God's merciful love is forever and is best understood through the lens of covenant. What is a covenant, and how does it help us understand his love?

A covenant is more than an impersonal contract in which two people agree to exchange goods or services. A covenant binds a person to another far beyond a mere legal contract. For example, the Sacrament of Matrimony has contractual and legal elements. But Matrimony is a covenant that binds two persons together for life. All covenants bind persons together in some way.

In Christ, God has established a new and eternal covenant with us. He has thus bound himself to us in a relationship of never-ending faithfulness and love. The nature of God's yearning for us reminds us that he longs for us to ask him for what we need the most. In fact, Jesus himself said, "Ask, and it will be given you; seek, and you will find; knock, and it will be opened to you. For every one who asks receives; and he who seeks finds; and to him who knocks it will be opened" (Matthew 7:7–8).

A few years ago, I had a rather personal and piercing experience of God in prayer. During the prayer experience, I found myself moved beyond words with gratitude for all God has done for me in my life. I remained in the space of gratitude for what seemed like forever, searching for the words to thank God for his absolute goodness to me. The emotion in my heart can only be described as profound gratitude and deep peace. However, as the prayer unfolded, I soon noticed a slight disturbance in my heart and asked the Lord what it might mean. He revealed to me that the disturbance was not mine but his. I was, at that moment, tasting in a small way the sadness in his heart regarding all the things he wanted to give me that I never asked for. Although I was so grateful for so much, this gratitude was not enough. God always longed to give me more. He longed for me to ask for more.

God longs for *you* to ask for more.

As we conclude our teaching on hearing God, my final encouragement to you is to ask. We do not ask enough. We do not ask for help as much as we should. We do not ask for the graces we need. I pray that you will ask God for help in hearing his voice every day for the rest of your life. Doing so daily will remind you of your desire for God and God's desire to give you the very thing you long for.

For Your Prayer

Read Matthew 7:7–11. Ask. Beg. Ask God for everything you long for.

What words stood out to you as you prayed?
What did you find stirring in your heart?

_____

_____

_____

_____

_____

_____

_____

_____

_____

_____

_____

_____

_____

_____

_____

_____

_____

_____

_____

_____

_____

Third Week — SATURDAY

Here are three questions to help you reflect on this week's meditations. You may find it helpful to discuss them with others or ponder them on your own before you begin the weekly reflection:

- Are you living in a balanced way? What is weighing you down or packing your schedule? How could living in a more balanced way help you hear God's desires for you?

- What are some concrete ways you can reset the rhythm of your day to be in harmony with God's Word? How can you rely more fully on him?

- **VIDEO REFLECTION:** How do you feel when you enter into prayer? What are the sensations, thoughts, and emotions you feel as you encounter silence? How can these feelings reveal something about your prayer and your relationship with God?

Now take a moment to reflect on the past week, going over the meditations that bore the most fruit in your prayer, the things you wrote, and your reflections on this week's video. How has your prayer changed this week?

_____

_____

_____

_____

_____

_____

_____

SUSCIPE PRAYER

Take, Lord, and receive all my liberty,
 my memory, my understanding,
 and my entire will,
 all I have and call my own.

You have given all to me.
 To you, Lord, I return it.

Everything is yours. Do with it what you will.
 Give me only your love and your grace.
 That is enough for me.

—St. Ignatius of Loyola

The Fourth Week of Advent

Enter In

First Reading

2 Samuel 7:1–5, 8b–12, 14a, 16

When King David was settled in his palace,
    and the LORD had given him rest from his enemies
      on every side,
    he said to Nathan the prophet,
    "Here I am living in a house of cedar,
    while the ark of God dwells in a tent!"
Nathan answered the king,
    "Go, do whatever you have in mind,
    for the LORD is with you."

But that night the LORD spoke to Nathan and said:
    "Go, tell my servant David, Thus says the LORD:
    Should you build me a house to dwell in?

"It was I who took you from the pasture
    and from the care of the flock
    to be commander of my people Israel.
I have been with you wherever you went,
    and I have destroyed all your enemies before you.
And I will make you famous like the great ones of
      the earth.

"I will fix a place for my people Israel;
    I will plant them so that they may dwell in their place
    without further disturbance.

Neither shall the wicked continue to afflict them as they
   did of old,
   since the time I first appointed judges over my
      people Israel.
I will give you rest from all your enemies.

"The LORD also reveals to you
   that he will establish a house for you.
And when your time comes and you rest with
      your ancestors,
   I will raise up your heir after you, sprung from
      your loins,
   and I will make his kingdom firm.

"I will be a father to him,
   and he shall be a son to me.
Your house and your kingdom shall endure forever
      before me;
   your throne shall stand firm forever."

Responsorial Psalm

Psalm 89:2-3, 4-5, 27, 29

R. *For ever I will sing the goodness of the Lord.*

The promises of the LORD I will sing forever;
   through all generations my mouth shall proclaim
      your faithfulness.
For you have said, "My kindness is established forever";
   in heaven you have confirmed your faithfulness.

"I have made a covenant with my chosen one,
 I have sworn to David my servant:
Forever will I confirm your posterity
 and establish your throne for all generations."

"He shall say of me, 'You are my father,
 my God, the Rock, my savior.'
Forever I will maintain my kindness toward him,
 and my covenant with him stands firm."

Second Reading

Romans 16:25-27

Brothers and sisters: To him who can strengthen you, according to my gospel and the proclamation of Jesus Christ, according to the revelation of the mystery kept secret for long ages but now manifested through the prophetic writings and, according to the command of the eternal God, made known to all nations to bring about the obedience of faith, to the only wise God, through Jesus Christ be glory forever and ever. Amen.

Gospel

Luke 1:26-38

The angel Gabriel was sent from God to a town of Galilee called Nazareth, to a virgin betrothed to a man named Joseph, of the house of David, and the virgin's name was Mary.

And coming to her, he said, "Hail, full of grace! The Lord is with you." But she was greatly troubled at what was said and pondered what sort of greeting this might be.

Then the angel said to her, "Do not be afraid, Mary, for you have found favor with God. Behold, you will conceive in your womb and bear a son, and you shall name him Jesus.

"He will be great and will be called Son of the Most High, and the Lord God will give him the throne of David his father, and he will rule over the house of Jacob forever, and of his kingdom there will be no end."

But Mary said to the angel, "How can this be, since I have no relations with a man?" And the angel said to her in reply, "The Holy Spirit will come upon you, and the power of the Most High will overshadow you. Therefore the child to be born will be called holy, the Son of God.

"And behold, Elizabeth, your relative, has also conceived a son in her old age, and this is the sixth month for her who was called barren; for nothing will be impossible for God." Mary said, "Behold, I am the handmaid of the Lord. May it be done to me according to your word." Then the angel departed from her.

Guided Meditations

A NOTE FROM FR. MARK

This final week of Advent will feel different from the first three weeks.

The daily meditations shift this week to guided, imaginative meditations designed to help us prepare more personally for Christmas. Why is this style of prayer important, and what exactly are we doing?

In his book *Meditation and Contemplation,* Fr. Tim Gallagher, OMV, writes, "In this manner of praying, Saint Ignatius tells us, we imaginatively *see the persons,* … we *hear the words* they speak, and we *observe the actions* they accomplish."*

I invite you to enter each guided meditation personally. Be *in* the scene. Be *with* the persons. Once the scene comes to its natural conclusion, when you feel God moving you along, simply share your heart with the Lord.

That said, this year's guided meditations differ from previous ones in the *Rejoice!* series. This is intentional. In the past, I invited you to imagine a scene almost as if you

---

* Timothy Gallagher, *Meditation and Contemplation: An Ignatian Guide to Praying with Scripture* (New York: Crossroad Publishing Company, 2008), 36, original emphasis.

were watching a movie, and then I invited you to enter that scene. Previously, guided meditations were intentionally written to teach you how to "do" imaginative prayer, and the focus was placed on the biblical character in the scene.

This year, I would like to take you one step deeper. This year you will notice that the guided meditations have *you* as the center of the meditation. Mary and Joseph are intentionally positioned in the meditation to help you remain at the center of the meditation. Why? Why would I do this?

In this year's *Rejoice!*, the theme of hearing God has anchored us for the first three weeks. If we are to hear God speak to *us,* we need to shift from simply reading the meditations to entering into them through our personal prayer. If we are to hear God speak to *us,* we do not need to "watch" the guided meditations as we watch a movie; instead, we must allow ourselves to be the person in the scene to whom the Lord speaks.

My prayer for you this week is that you allow the Lord to take you deeper. The Lord wants to speak to *you.* May this week and its guided meditations intentionally enable you to hear the voice of the Lord.

MARY

"Behold, I am the

handmaid of the Lord;

let it be to me according

to your word."

—Luke 1:38

FIND A QUIET PLACE

to pray today, a place where you will be uninterrupted and without distractions for about fifteen minutes. Once there, read all the way through today's mediation. Then close your eyes and imagine everything described in the meditation. Ask the Holy Spirit to help you pray.

Invoking the simple authority given to you at your baptism, ask the Lord to bless your mind so that you may know his mysteries. Ask him to bless your ears so that you may hear his voice, to bless your eyes so that you may see his presence, and to bless your lips so that you may speak his praise. Ask the Lord to bless your heart so that you may know his love.

Close your eyes and, using your imagination, visualize yourself sitting in the very place you are sitting now. Take a few moments to see your surroundings in your mind's eye. In your imagination, let yourself see what's around you. Let yourself feel the things you can touch. Notice the things you can smell and hear. Ask the Holy Spirit to guide your prayer.

***

Now imagine that the door opens into the room where you are sitting. Visualize the door opening and someone walking through it. It is Mary, the Blessed Mother, the wife of Joseph. As she enters the room, she turns and walks toward you. She stands in front of you and gazes into your eyes, beholding you as you are. Then she sits beside you.

Look at Mary. In your imagination, visualize what she looks like—her hair, her face, and her eyes. What are her eyes like?

Take a few moments to imagine what Mary is like and simply look at her. Let her look at you.

As you sit with her, ask her to describe what it was like for her to hear the angel speak to her in the Annunciation. Ask her to tell you why she was afraid at the beginning of that conversation. What it was like for her to be told she would conceive the Messiah in her womb? What it was like to say yes and surrender to God's plan? Listen to her.

Imagine now that Mary touches your shoulder, inviting silence and prayer. Ask God to speak to you, and listen in silence. Is God asking something of you as he asked something of Mary? God had a very specific invitation for Mary, and she said yes. At this stage of your life, is God asking something of you? If so, what is it? What do you want to say in reply?

Listen deeply in your heart. Perhaps you will hear a subtle voice within. Perhaps Mary will say something to you on God's behalf. You may be led to a particular Bible passage or feel a particular sensation in your body. There are various ways in which God may try to speak to you.

After you have spent a few moments listening to the voice of God, return to Mary's presence with you. Stay there as long as you desire or as long as her presence remains with you.

As you conclude, pray any words of thanksgiving that rise from your heart.

**What was your experience of prayer today?
What did you find stirring in your heart?**

_____

_____

_____

_____

_____

_____

_____

_____

_____

_____

_____

_____

_____

_____

_____

_____

_____

_____

_____

_____

_____

Fourth Week — MEDITATION ONE

JOSEPH

"When Joseph woke from sleep, he did as the angel of the Lord commanded him."

—Matthew 1:24

AS YOU DID YESTERDAY,

find a quiet place to pray today, a place where you will be uninterrupted and without distractions for about fifteen minutes. Once there, read all the way through today's mediation. Then close your eyes and imagine everything described in the meditation. Ask the Holy Spirit to help you pray.

Invoking the simple authority given to you at your baptism, ask the Lord to bless your mind so that you may know his mysteries. Ask him to bless your ears so that you may hear his voice, to bless your eyes so that you may see his presence, and to bless your lips so that you may speak his praise. Ask the Lord to bless your heart so that you may know his love.

Close your eyes and, using your imagination, visualize yourself sitting in the very place you are sitting now. Take a few moments to see your surroundings in your mind's eye. In your imagination, let yourself see what's around you. Let yourself feel the things you can touch. Notice the things you can smell and hear. Ask the Holy Spirit to guide your prayer.

***

Now imagine that the door opens into the room where you are sitting. Visualize the door opening and someone walking through it. It is St. Joseph. As he enters the room, he turns and walks toward you. He looks at you with a gentle spirit, and as he sits beside you, warmth radiates from his person. Look at St. Joseph. Imagine what he looks like. Visualize his hair, his beard, his face, and his eyes. What is he like in your imagination? How do you feel in his presence? Take a few moments to visualize what St. Joseph is like. Be with him. _____

As you sit with him, ask him to describe the dream he had before Jesus' birth, when the angel spoke to him the first time. Ask him why he was afraid to take Mary, his wife, into his home. Ask him to describe what it was like to hear the angel say that Mary was pregnant with the Messiah. Ask him to describe what was in his heart when he said yes to God's plan.

Imagine now that St. Joseph places his hand on your shoulder, inviting silence and prayer. Ask God to speak to you, and listen in silence. Is God asking you to trust as he asked Joseph to trust? How and where do you need to trust? What is in your heart as you ponder the invitation to trust?

As you did yesterday, take a few moments to listen. Remember that there are various ways that God may speak to you.

After you have spent a few moments listening to the voice of God, return to Joseph's presence with you. Stay there as long as you desire or as long as he remains with you.

As you conclude, pray any words of thanksgiving that rise from your heart.

What was your experience of prayer today?
What did you find stirring in your heart?

AFRAID

" Perfect love
casts out fear. "

—1 John 4:18

FIND A QUIET PLACE

to pray as you did yesterday, a place where you will be uninterrupted and without distractions for about fifteen minutes. Once there, read all the way through today's mediation. Then close your eyes and imagine everything described in the meditation. Ask the Holy Spirit to help you pray.

Invoking the simple authority given to you at your baptism, ask the Lord to bless your mind so that you may know his mysteries. Ask him to bless your ears so that you may hear his voice, to bless your eyes so that you may see his presence, and to bless your lips so that you may speak his praise. Ask the Lord to bless your heart so that you may know his love.

Close your eyes and, using your imagination, visualize yourself sitting in the very place you are sitting now. Take a few moments to see your surroundings in your mind's eye. In your imagination, let yourself see what's around you. Let yourself feel the things you can touch. Notice the things you can smell and hear. Ask the Holy Spirit to guide your prayer.

***

Now imagine that the door opens into the room where you are sitting. Visualize the door opening and both Mary and Joseph entering the room. They walk toward you and then sit in front of you. They both look at you with love, and you can feel their happiness in being with you.

Imagine that Mary looks you in the eye and begins to tell you about all she was afraid of during that first Advent. Imagine that she speaks to you about her fear of what Joseph would say, what her parents would say, and what people would think about her pregnancy before joining Joseph in their home. Ask the Holy Spirit to help you hear Mary's voice as she tells you about her fear.

Imagine then that Joseph does the same. He tells you about the things he was afraid of during that first Advent. Imagine that he speaks to you about his fear of Mary's conceiving the long-awaited Messiah, his fear of having to model fatherhood for God's Son, and his fear of living up to such an awesome task. Ask the Holy Spirit to help you hear Joseph's voice as he tells you about his fears.

Now imagine that Joseph and Mary each place a hand on your shoulder, inviting silence and prayer. Ask God to speak to you, and listen in silence. What are you afraid of at this stage of your life? Is there anything you fear in your past, present, or future? Spend a few moments in silence, and ask God to reveal any fear you might have. If God places something in your heart, talk to him as you would talk to your best friend. Share with God everything that is in your heart about the fear. Then listen once again to his reply.

After listening to the voice of God, return to the presence of Mary and Joseph with you. Stay there as long as you desire or as long as they remain with you.

As you conclude, pray any words of thanksgiving that rise from your heart.

What was your experience of prayer today?
What did you find stirring in your heart?

_____

_____

_____

_____

_____

_____

_____

_____

_____

_____

_____

_____

_____

_____

_____

_____

_____

_____

_____

_____

UNKNOWN

" Fear not, little flock, for
it is your Father's good
pleasure to give you
the kingdom. "

—Luke 12:32

FIND A QUIET PLACE

to pray as you did yesterday, a place where you will be uninterrupted and without distractions for about fifteen minutes. Once there, read all the way through today's mediation. Then close your eyes and imagine everything described in the meditation. Ask the Holy Spirit to help you pray.

Invoking the simple authority given to you at your baptism, ask the Lord to bless your mind so that you may know his mysteries. Ask him to bless your ears so that you may hear his voice, to bless your eyes so that you may see his presence, and to bless your lips so that you may speak his praise. Ask the Lord to bless your heart so that you may know his love.

Close your eyes and, using your imagination, visualize yourself sitting in the very place you are sitting now. Take a few moments to see your surroundings in your mind's eye. In your imagination, let yourself see what's around you. Let yourself feel the things you can touch. Notice the things you can smell and hear. Ask the Holy Spirit to guide your prayer.

***

Now imagine that the door opens into the room where you are sitting. Visualize the door opening and both Mary and Joseph entering the room. They walk toward you and then sit in front of you. They both look at you with love, and you can feel their happiness in being with you.

Imagine that Mary looks you in the eye and begins speaking to you about all that was unknown in her life during that first Advent. Imagine that she speaks to you about the new experiences of being pregnant, preparing to become a mother, and delivering a baby.

Ask the Holy Spirit to keep guiding your imagination, and visualize Joseph as he too looks you in the eye and speaks to you about the unknowns in his life during that first Advent. He tells you about not knowing what people would think of Mary's pregnancy, about becoming a father, and about dealing with the difficulty of finding shelter for Mary in Bethlehem.

Now imagine that Joseph and Mary each place a hand on your shoulder, inviting your silence and prayer. Ask God to speak to you, and listen in silence. Where are there unknowns in your life? Are you facing anything now with unknown circumstances, present or future? What is your response to the unknown? If God places something in your heart, speak to him as you would speak to your best friend. Share with God everything that is in your heart about the unknown. Then listen once again to his reply.

After listening to the voice of God, return to Mary and Joseph's presence with you. Stay there as long as you desire or as long as they are with you.

As you conclude, pray any words of thanksgiving that rise from your heart.

What was your experience of prayer today?
What did you find stirring in your heart?

_____

_____

_____

_____

_____

_____

_____

_____

_____

_____

_____

_____

_____

_____

_____

_____

_____

_____

_____

_____

NEED

> **"Your Father knows what you need before you ask him."**

—Luke 6:8

FIND A QUIET PLACE

to pray as you did yesterday, a place where you will be uninterrupted and without distractions for about fifteen minutes. Once there, read all the way through today's mediation. Then close your eyes and imagine everything described in the meditation. Ask the Holy Spirit to help you pray.

Invoking the simple authority given to you at your baptism, ask the Lord to bless your mind so that you may know his mysteries. Ask him to bless your ears so that you may hear his voice, to bless your eyes so that you may see his presence, and to bless your lips so that you may speak his praise. Ask the Lord to bless your heart so that you may know his love.

Close your eyes and, using your imagination, visualize yourself sitting in the very place you are sitting now. Take a few moments to see your surroundings in your mind's eye. In your imagination, let yourself see what's around you. Let yourself feel the things you can touch. Notice the things you can smell and hear. Ask the Holy Spirit to guide your prayer.

***

Now imagine that the door opens into the room where you are sitting. Visualize the door opening and someone walking through the door. It is Mary. As she enters the room, she turns and walks toward you. She stands in front of you and gazes into your eyes, beholding you as you are. Then she sits beside you.

Look at Mary. In your imagination, visualize what she looks like—her hair, her face, and her eyes. What are her eyes like in your imagination? Take a few moments to imagine what Mary is like, and simply look at her. Let her look at you. _____

As she sits with you, Mary begins to tell you about all she needed from God during that first Advent. Ask the Holy Spirit to guide your imagination as she speaks about her physical needs—her fatigue and need for rest, her need to accept her vulnerability and to accept help with things she could ordinarily do on her own, and her need for patience with the discomforts of traveling on a donkey over the many miles to Bethlehem. Ask the Holy Spirit to guide your imagination as she speaks to you about her interior needs as well, especially how she needed to trust God without knowing exactly how things would unfold. Listen as she tells you how she interceded for Joseph throughout his struggle. Listen as she shares her need for wisdom since she had no experience as an expectant mother.

Now imagine that Mary places a hand on your shoulder, inviting silence and prayer. Ask God to speak to you, and listen in silence. Christmas is right around the corner. What do you need from God this Christmas?

After listening to the voice of God, return to Mary's presence with you. Stay there as long as you desire or as long as she remains with you.

As you conclude, pray any words of thanksgiving that rise from your heart.

What was your experience of prayer today?
What did you find stirring in your heart?

_____

_____

_____

_____

_____

_____

_____

_____

_____

_____

_____

_____

_____

_____

_____

_____

_____

_____

_____

_____

HELP

"Trust in the LORD
with all your heart,
and do not rely on
your own insight.
In all your ways
acknowledge him,
and he will make
straight your paths."

—Proverbs 3:5–6

AS YOU DID YESTERDAY,

find a quiet place to pray today, a place where you will be uninterrupted and without distractions for about fifteen minutes. Once there, read all the way through today's mediation. Then close your eyes and imagine everything described in the meditation. Ask the Holy Spirit to help you pray.

Invoking the simple authority given to you at your baptism, ask the Lord to bless your mind so that you may know his mysteries. Ask him to bless your ears so that you may hear his voice, to bless your eyes so that you may see his presence, and to bless your lips so that you may speak his praise. Ask the Lord to bless your heart so that you may know his love.

Close your eyes and, using your imagination, visualize yourself sitting in the very place you are sitting now. Take a few moments to see your surroundings in your mind's eye. In your imagination, let yourself see what's around you. Let yourself feel the things you can touch. Notice the things you can smell and hear. Ask the Holy Spirit to guide your prayer.

***

Now imagine that the door opens into the room where you are sitting. Visualize the door opening and someone walking through the door. It is Joseph. As he enters the room, he turns and walks toward you. He stands in front of you and gazes into your eyes, beholding you as you are. Then he sits beside you.

Look at Joseph. Imagine what he looks like. Visualize his hair, his face, and his eyes. What are his eyes like in your imagination? Take a few moments to visualize what Joseph is like, and simply look at him. Let him look at you.

As he sits with you, Joseph begins to tell you about all he needed from God during that first Advent, especially his need to trust God as he considered his future role in Jesus' life. Ask the Holy Spirit to guide your imagination as Joseph speaks to you about his physical needs—his fatigue during the journey to Bethlehem and his hunger because they had so little food. Ask the Holy Spirit to guide your imagination as he speaks to you about his interior needs as well, especially how he needed to trust that they would find a suitable place for Jesus' birth.

Now imagine that Joseph places a hand on your shoulder, inviting silence and prayer. Ask God to speak to you, and listen in silence. Again, Christmas is right around the corner. What do you need from God this Christmas? Specifically, where or how do you need help?

After listening to the voice of God, return to Joseph's presence with you. Stay there as long as you desire or as long as he remains with you.

As you conclude, pray any words of thanksgiving that rise from your heart.

What was your experience of prayer today?
What did you find stirring in your heart?

_____

_____

_____

_____

_____

_____

_____

_____

_____

_____

_____

_____

_____

_____

_____

_____

_____

_____

_____

_____

_____

_____

_____

_____

WOMB

"Henceforth all generations
will call me blessed;
for he who is mighty has
done great things for me,
and holy is his name."

—Luke 1:48–49

AS YOU'VE DONE

throughout the week, find a quiet place to pray today, a place where you will be uninterrupted and without distractions for about fifteen minutes. Once there, read all the way through today's mediation. Then close your eyes and imagine everything described in the meditation. Ask the Holy Spirit to help you pray.

Invoking the simple authority given to you at your baptism, ask the Lord to bless your mind so that you may know his mysteries. Ask him to bless your ears so that you may hear his voice, to bless your eyes so that you may see his presence, and to bless your lips so that you may speak his praise. Ask the Lord to bless your heart so that you may know his love.

Close your eyes and, using your imagination, visualize yourself sitting in the very place you are sitting now. Take a few moments to see your surroundings in your mind's eye. In your imagination, let yourself see what's around you. Let yourself feel the things you can touch. Notice the things you can smell and hear. Ask the Holy Spirit to guide your prayer.

***

Now imagine that the door opens into the room where you are sitting. Visualize the door opening and both Mary and Joseph entering the room. They walk toward you and then sit down in front of you. They both look at you with love, and you can feel their happiness in being with you.

Imagine what Mary looks like one day before giving birth to her son. Mary sits just a few feet away from you. Her garments are a dignified veil for the beauty of her womb. There, in that womb, in her womb, lives the Savior of the world.

Now imagine Mary standing and taking a few steps to be closer to you. Imagine that she takes one of your hands and places it lightly on her belly. You can feel the rough fabric of her dress. You know that within her is the womb where God lives. What is it like for you to touch her in this way? God, the Almighty himself, is in *this* womb.

Pause for a moment and listen. Ask the Lord to speak to you. After listening to the voice of God, return to Mary and Joseph's presence with you. Stay there as long as you desire or as long as they remain with you.

As you conclude, pray any words of thanksgiving that rise from your heart.

What was your experience of prayer today?
What did you find stirring in your heart?

_____

_____

_____

_____

_____

_____

_____

_____

_____

_____

_____

_____

_____

_____

_____

_____

_____

_____

_____

_____

LITANY OF HUMILITY

Lord Jesus, meek and humble of heart, hear me.

From the desire of being esteemed,
deliver me, Jesus.

From the desire of being loved,
deliver me, Jesus.

From the desire of being extolled,
deliver me, Jesus.

From the desire of being honored,
deliver me, Jesus.

From the desire of being praised,
deliver me, Jesus.

From the desire of being preferred to others,
deliver me, Jesus.

From the desire of being consulted,
deliver me, Jesus.

From the desire of being approved,
deliver me, Jesus.

From the fear of being humiliated,
    deliver me, Jesus.

From the fear of being despised,
    deliver me, Jesus.

From the fear of suffering rebukes,
    deliver me, Jesus.

From the fear of being calumniated,
    deliver me, Jesus.

From the fear of being forgotten,
    deliver me, Jesus.

From the fear of being ridiculed,
    deliver me, Jesus.

From the fear of being wronged,
    deliver me, Jesus.

From the fear of being suspected,
    deliver me, Jesus.

That others may be loved more than I,
Jesus, grant me the grace to desire it.

That others may be esteemed more than I,
Jesus, grant me the grace to desire it.

That in the opinion of the world, others may increase and
I may decrease,
Jesus, grant me the grace to desire it.

That others may be chosen and I set aside,
Jesus, grant me the grace to desire it.

That others may be praised and I unnoticed,
Jesus, grant me the grace to desire it.

That others may be preferred to me in everything,
Jesus, grant me the grace to desire it.

That others may become holier than I, provided that I
may become as holy as I should,
Jesus, grant me the grace to desire it.

—Cardinal Rafael Merry del Val (1865–1930)

HEAR

"Be not afraid; for behold, I
bring you good news of
a great joy which will
come to all the people;
for to you is born this day
in the city of David
a Savior, who is
Christ the Lord."

—Luke 2:10–11

AS YOU DID YESTERDAY,

find a quiet place to pray today, a place where you will be uninterrupted and without distractions for about fifteen minutes. Once there, read all the way through today's mediation. Then close your eyes and imagine everything described in the meditation. Ask the Holy Spirit to help you pray.

Invoking the simple authority given to you at your baptism, ask the Lord to bless your mind so that you may know his mysteries. Ask him to bless your ears so that you may hear his voice, to bless your eyes so that you may see his presence, and to bless your lips so that you may speak his praise. Ask the Lord to bless your heart so that you may know his love.

Close your eyes and, using your imagination, visualize yourself sitting in the very place you are sitting now. Take a few moments to see your surroundings in your mind's eye. In your imagination, let yourself see what's around you. Let yourself feel the things you can touch. Notice the things you can smell and hear. Ask the Holy Spirit to guide your prayer.

***

Now imagine that the door opens into the room where you are sitting. Visualize the door opening and both Mary and Joseph entering the room. However, something is different today. Today *three* people enter the room—for they are holding a baby! As they enter the room, they sit in front of you. They look at you with love, and you can feel their happiness in being with you.

Imagine what Mary looks like the morning after giving birth to her son. She sits just a few feet away from you and beams with joy. Her smile radiates the inexpressible joy of holding, in *her* arms, the Son of God.

Now imagine the sounds that break into the silence. You hear the baby. You hear the cooing of the newborn infant. That sound, that voice, is the infant voice of God. In Jesus, God is not invisible. In him, God now has a name. God now has a face and a voice. The voice of this child will eventually speak the words of the Gospel and the Good News of the kingdom. Imagine that you hear *that* voice.

Pause for a moment and listen. Ask the Lord to speak to you. After listening to the voice of God, return to the Holy Family's presence with you. Stay there as long as you desire or as long as they remain with you.

As you conclude, pray any words of thanksgiving that rise from your heart.

What was your experience of prayer today?
What did you find stirring in your heart?

_____

_____

_____

_____

_____

_____

_____

_____

_____

_____

_____

_____

_____

_____

_____

_____

_____

_____

_____

_____

CHRISTMAS DAY MEDITATION

Here are three questions to help you reflect on this week's meditations. You may find it helpful to discuss them with others or ponder them on your own before you begin the weekly reflection:

- What are you taking from this Advent into the rest of your life? What lessons did you learn, what fruit did your prayer bear, how did you notice God speaking to you?

- How did sitting with Mary and Joseph this week prepare you to meet Jesus on Christmas Day?

- VIDEO REFLECTION: Do you think it is impossible to have silence in your state in life? What are you putting ahead of prayer and silence? How can you make the space and take the time to sit with the Lord in stillness?

Take a moment to reflect on the whole of Advent and Christmas, going over the meditations that bore the most fruit in your prayer, the things you wrote, and your reflections on the videos. How has your prayer changed this Advent?

Thank God for what he is doing in your life. Thank him for the extraordinary gift of his Son.

_____

_____

_____

_____

_____

"And the Word became flesh and dwelt among us, full of grace and truth."

—John 1:14

Credits

Executive Producer
Jonathan Strate

General Manager
Jeffrey Cole, Lauren McCann

Product Manager and Content Manager
Julia Coppa Bernetsky, Lauren Welsh

Project Manager
Veronica Salazar

Editorial
Rebecca Robinson, Christina Eberle, Brady Beckerman

Graphics
Stella Ziegler, Sarah Stueve

Video
Matt Pirrall, Ellie Spencer, Worklight Pictures

Marketing
Mark Leopold, Julia Amting

About the Author

Ordained in 2001, Fr. Mark Toups is known for his joyful, encouraging spiritual advice as he helps Catholics develop habits of daily prayer. His many books and studies with Ascension serve as valued resources for Catholics to deepen their prayer lives and encounter the Lord in meaningful ways, particularly through meditation on the Scriptures and through celebration of the seasons of Advent and Lent.

Fr. Toups is a priest for the Diocese of Houma-Thibodaux, where he is the vicar general for the diocese and the pastor of Our Lady of the Isle in Grand Isle, Louisiana. In addition to his pastoral work, Fr. Toups is an adjunct faculty member for the Institute for Priestly Formation, specializing in communications, development, and spiritual direction. Fr. Toups received his master of divinity (MDiv) degree from Notre Dame Seminary in New Orleans. A graduate of Nicholls State University, he is a native of Houma, Louisiana.

Fr. Toups is the author of *Oremus: A Catholic Guide to Prayer*, the *Rejoice!* Advent Meditations series, and *The Ascension Lenten Companion* series from Ascension.

About the Illustrator

Mike Moyers has illustrated *Rejoice!* and *The Ascension Lenten Companion* since both series began six years ago, capturing in them the beauty and wonder of the lives of Jesus, Mary, and Joseph and those they loved. His paintings present the Holy Family and other figures from Scripture in a more human way so they no longer feel like characters in a story but real people. "We are witnesses of God's wonders," he says.

Mike begins a painting by reading and praying with a Bible story, imagining the details. Then, he says, "I have to let God take it from there." His paintings thus often capture the in-between moments of familiar stories—quiet and tender gestures that we know must have happened along the way. He purposely keeps some details vague to make space for the Holy Spirit, so what we see can be shaped by a deeper vision. His hope is "that people will continue to enjoy and receive God's grace through the paintings I make."

He lives with his wife and children in Franklin, Tennessee. See more of his work at mikemoyersfineart.com.

Learn more about Mike's journey and the faith that inspires him:

Find the **videos** and **other resources** for this *Rejoice!* journal at **RejoiceProgram.com.**

Rejoice! program essentials:

- Free videos for each week of Advent from the author, Fr. Mark Toups, with Fr. Josh Johnson and Sr. Josephine Garrett
- Free downloads for your parish: poster, pulpit announcement, flyer, and bulletin announcement

Other resources:

- Advent prayer cards for praying with your Advent wreath
- *Rejoice!* art prints, available on museum-quality paper or canvas
- **NEW** *Rejoice!* Christmas cards
- **NEW** *Rejoice!* Christmas ornaments